Thanks to

Brian Ross, Earl of Sandwich, Gray's School of Art, and
our collaborators at the Centre for Modern Thought.

I0483610

Recoded
Landscapes and Politics of New Media.

Recoded: A User's Manual

It is increasingly a matter of daily conversation and mainstream concern – "UK risks drift to surveillance society, say MPs"-- reads a headline on Yahoo! News.[1] A month prior it is reported that the British Home Office has plans for a database holding records of each and every phone call, email, and time spent on the Internet by the public as part of its "war" against crime and terrorism, a plan that would require the government manage literally billions of records (given that text messages alone in Britain in 2007 totalled 57 billion).[2] Meanwhile, the U.S. Department of Homeland Security announces that visitors from all the visa waiver countries, including the UK, must register 72 hours ahead of departing, as "the latest measure to strengthen American security."[3]

Already responding to this environment of the omniscience of the mass media, if not yet mass surveillance, demonstrations in Paris in the 1980s often rejected placards or slogans, refusing that their demands be mediatised. A more passive response would be that of the fictional students in Bertrand Bonello's film *The Pornographer* (2001), whose call to protest is "Be Mute." Fumbling for terms, perhaps, Net pundits Alexander R. Galloway and Eugene Thacker propose "non-existence," calling for a way of being that will elude the "measurable science of control," and any representable identity, writing that "the non-existent is that which cannot be parsed by any available algorithms,"[4] itself a strategy that seems to merely reprise the fugitive activism of Hakim Bey's "temporary autonomous zones" of over fifteen years ago.[5]

Theorist Susan Buck-Morss has written about the phenomenon of "disappearance" of artists, where they do not so much provide public art for the community, but rather the community provides "public sanctuary for the artist."[6] Speaking of a 2000 exhibition she helped curate, she writes that artists "escaped temporarily from the conditions of being-in-the-artworld, moving into the sheltering hybridity of border communities in a way that defined public art less as an avant-garde than as an underground."[7] Increasingly, experimenting with these new identities, or non-identities, artists like Trevor Paglen and Jill Magid, or the protagonist of William Gibson's novel *Spook Country* (2007), take on counter-surveillance as their artistic mandate. The exhibition *Recoded: Landscapes and Politics of New Media*, is one attempt to make sense of this wide and fluid territory, and of artistic responses to it.

In answer to a question in Philadelphia in 1960, Marcel Duchamp replied, "In the future, artists will have to be underground."[8] At about the same time, Glaswegian novelist Alexander Trocchi promulgated the Situationist call for an "invisible insurrection of a million minds." By 1968, French writer Jean Genet, in the middle of the raucous media spectacle and "police riot" of the Democratic convention, came to the conclusion that "There is no reality in

America. Too many cameras."[9] They all seemed to prophesise the current onrushing hypertrophy of the visual and proliferating media of all sorts, from webcams to cellphone movies, to cab rides with television where hardly any single moment is untouched by mediation, by what Agent Mulder in the TV show *The X-Files*, in a valiant attempt many years ago to 'name the system,' dubbed "the military-industrial-entertainment complex." With the remarkable levels of television viewing and web surfing alone, one would think "Big Brother" functioned merely through people watching their various media boxes – the public watches the media, and thus distracted, the government doesn't need to watch the public.

Yet the "information revolution" and the vaunted freedom of borders promised by 'globalisation,' have seen a vast, unprecedented extension of mass government surveillance, in what author Naomi Klein has called "a bizarre merger of security and shopping cultures." [10] Numerous devices used for marketing to consumers deemed too scary before September 11, such as biometric ID cards and optical scanning, are rapidly accepted as part of the "War on Terror." It is an extraordinarily profitable arrangement where nominally "private" corporations ally with "emergency" or authoritarian state practices of the "public" sector as if hand in glove. The planned electronic/security fence along the U.S./Mexico border, for instance, is worth $2.5 billion to Boeing and its allied consortium.[11] This is not to ignore the vast new business opportunities in data mining and information management, since, with the explosion of forms of surveillance – whether of financial records, web surfing, phone calls, snail mail, or by old-fashioned wiretapping – the governments of the world are literally "drowning in data,"[12] and often at a loss of how to map it.[13]

There is no denying that this is an ultimate "growth industry." In New York City, one can expect to be surveilled an average of 77 times on any given day. While Scotland has plans to catch up with England in number of CCTVs, where there is now one camera for every fourteen people, the city of Shenzhen, China ups the ante – within three years it will have a camera for every six people, making it the most surveilled city on the planet.[14] Shenzhen is the picture of at least one putative future, already present. Here, one of China's first "special economic zones," what was only thirty years ago a string of fishing villages and collectively farmed rice paddies has blossomed into a city of 12.4 million people and 100,000 factories. An economic and social experiment in largely unregulated capitalism, its cameras are part of another experiment, one in surveillance and censorship known as Golden Shield. Aided by the latest technology from U.S.-based corporations such as IBM, Honeywell, and General Electric, Shenzhen's cameras will be linked to all the other forms of surveillance – the Internet, phones, GPS monitors, facial-recognition software – while the population's movement will also be monitored through national ID cards with scannable computer chips and photos that are instantly uploaded into police databases. Golden Shield envisages a comprehensive, massive database, ranging from biometrics to work history, for each person in China - 1.3 billion people. The goal is to have one centralised surveillance system, linked from city to city, and extending even into the countryside. One of the first tests of this system has just recently come and gone, where it passed with flying colours.

As Klein reports, when the protests in Tibet erupted on March 14, 2008, in an instant "every supposedly liberating tool of the information age - mobile phones, satellite TV, the internet - was transformed into a method of repression and control."[15] Mobilizing the "Great Firewall," the Chinese government blocked with ease foreign news outlets, phone and mobile calls, blitzed mobiles with messages from the police, and shut down sections of the Internet altogether. Tibet is filled with surveillance cameras, up to and including motion-detecting devices in monastery prayer rooms. During the uprising, the Chinese government compiled some of the most violent footage of the demonstrators for round the clock viewing on state television, while the surveillance footage also furnished mugshots of protestors fed into the national database, and broadcast as "WANTED" on all Chinese news stations, resulting within days in hundreds of arrests. When the designers of this system claim their models to be present-day London and Bush administration America, they are only being honest.

These recent events seem custom-made to reveal Galloway and Thacker's thesis, that "codification, not reification" is the order of the day, to be accurate. No longer is only giving up one's body in the form of labour power the form of exploitation, as in industrial society, but also the information of one's body, for various forms of classification and control, as in various forms of post-industrial or 'information' society. In trying to define what philosopher Gilles Deleuze described as the "ultrarapid forms of apparently free-floating control"[16] in newly coalescing "control" societies, Galloway has provided a kind of taxonomy of how such codification works, through its specified "protocols." The Internet, for example, is eminently protocological in that it combines, in uneasy balance, on the one hand an extreme distribution of "control" into horizontal, autonomous bodies and forms, and on the other, a vertical hierarchisation of "wrappers" and layers of command that make such distribution possible.

As Galloway writes, a protocol is a "distributed management system that allows control to exist within a heterogeneous material milieu."[17] The Internet, for instance, provides only an illusion of the absence of centralised control and command, characteristic of the new "diagram of distribution."

That protocols are materially immanent, are endogenous, that is, do not follow a model of command from outside their system, does not make them less effective, - quite the contrary.[18] It follows for Galloway that any resistance has to be predicated on this protocological reality. This can be a laser beam pointed directly at a surveillance camera blinding it, or myriad tactics of exodus, a non-appearance linked to a fuller being of freedom.[19] It remains to be seen, given Galloway's preference to "blackbox economics,"[20] whether the protocological priority focuses sufficiently on the origin of exploitation and domination, whether concentration on the form of protocol occludes or supports a wider, sufficient political vision.

In what has been a wave of group activity in the past decade and more, collectives like Kein Mensch ist illegal, Bureau d'Etudes, or Institute for Applied Autonomy, Bureau of Inverse Technology, Yo Mango, the Yes Men, Electronic Disturbance Theater, and Critical Art Ensemble, move in and out of strictly 'art' contexts, where the visibility or invisibility of the artist is provisional, depending on context and situation, the tactics to be employed, the rollcall of participants and the languages to be used.[21] The art of making protocological process highly visible, on the other hand, is well present in *Recoded*. Critical strategies that defamiliarise, de- and re-contextualise, *détourne* and hijack, counter-surveil and counter-map. That one work was deemed not "aesthetic" enough for one institution in Aberdeen to display, signals an unintended tribute to this heuristic confusion.

Jens Strandberg explores how Power Point "naturalises" the display of information, and forces a narrative that leaves as little room as possible for "flux between the slides and subjects," thereby suggesting "what kind of information we present," and producing what design critic Edward Tufte has called "relentless sequentiality."[22] An eminently protocological critique, Strandberg's research project leads him to Power Point's various ideological applications, from Colin Powell's now infamous February 2003 UN speech, to Power Point's use as the program of choice for much of the American Christian evangelical movement. For others this process can involve a playful inversion, or *ju-jitsu* of imposed media.

Plan b (Sophia New and Daniel Belasco Rogers) use GPS and PDA technology to map their peregrinations in various cities, whether Bristol or Berlin, mapping their relationship that shifts as well as that between sound, visuals, narrative, and space. With their "locative soundscapes" they place stories back in the environment that gave rise to them. A kind of "psychogeography" but far less assuming than the Situationist "drift" or *dérive*, plan b offers up a counter-modeling to the hylomorphism of city planners and its moulding of experience. Opting for a ludic alternative to putatively public space, in *The Duellists* (2007) David Valentine captures, using the in-house CCTV camera network at the Arndale shopping centre in Manchester, the "free-running" of the parkour "breakin' crew" Methods of Movement. Using the emptied shopping centre as their stage, Methods of Movement enact a dance resounding in the halls of abandoned consumerism. A product of collaboration with the free media space Mediashed, *The Duellists* is also the first use of the free media/ video toolkit 'Gearbox,' developed with Eyebeam Studios in New York, as DIY increasingly keeps pace with events. In a similar DIY spirit Alexander Egger pursues in his zines the fragile and the fragmentary, the cast-off and fugitive, the detritus of everyday life – fleeting moments and phrases, dreams and impressions deliberately unpackaged, presented in minimal format, in their very anonymity vying for attention in a clamouring, hi-tech world.

This concern with contagion, as well as following the call for what Fredric Jameson decades ago dubbed "cognitive mapping," is part of the mission of the collective RYbN, with their anti-data mining project and installation. A response to the visualisation and virtualisation of data in protean, well-nigh overwhelming forms, RYbN seeks to re-present the various flows – whether social, economic political, financial or cultural – into a new cartography. Another example of fruitful "discipline jumping," RYbN's performance/installation is at once real-time performance, geopolitical and economic commentary, and artistic research. In league with artists such as Mark Lombardi, Ursula Biemann, or Bureau d'Études, they seek to re-materialise what is so often ballyhooed as a ghostly or "immaterial" process. By diverting the tools of the new information and surveillance order, they provide another face and experience to it.

Similarly, skúta, with his installation "Happy Feet in Aberdeen," plays with the dialectic of what is visible and what is invisible, repositioning surveillance cameras from authoritative "bird's eye" view to deferential "child's eye" view, and establishing a "live surveillance exchange" between the Earl of Sandwich shop and the Peacock Visual Arts gallery, where people at the sandwich shop view the fruits of the cameras at the other location, disrupting the assumption that the surveillance is of their own location. An exercise that prompts social and protocological awareness, skúta's work also operates in the interstices of 'public' and 'private,' a boundary surveillance is duty-bound to cross. Anna Jermolaewa's video *Ass Peeping* (2003) also inverts private/public in her open display of voyeurism, again questioning what is "naturalised" in a society so based on the visible.

One of the more dramatic forays into giving a "face" to the goings on of surveillance society has been the work of Trevor Paglen. Characteristically inter-disciplinary, Paglen works between geography,

investigative journalism, social science, contemporary art, and practices such as limit telephotography, that enables photography of landscapes invisible to an unaided eye. Not content to only read of reports of "extraordinary rendition," the program where the U.S. Central Intelligence Agency (CIA) trundles off suspects to remote and secret prisons to be tortured in interrogations, Paglen photographed such bases in Afghanistan. Part of a wave of artists that take up the hope of author/activist Mark LaVine of "combining cutting-edge research and equally cutting-edge art with innovative forms of progressive social activism,"[23] Paglen along with journalist A.C. Thompson has documented his rendition investigations in the book *Torture Taxi* (2007). The results of this research and other investigations into secret military installations are displayed as blurry photographs of secret bases, and a series of fake signatures of functionaries of CIA "proprietary companies."

Caleb Larsen takes another tack to visualisation. Larsen has linked a computer program which scans headlines of 4,500 English language news sources to a ceiling-mounted mechanism. With an algorithm determining the number of deaths reported in each news item, the program prompts the mechanism to release one yellow BB for each death, the evidence accumulating on the floor. Larsen's concern with the interface of "invisible" or "immaterial" digital means with "visible" physical manifestation, in this case a kinetic sculpture, and cartography of current events, places him in the middle of an exhibition like *Recoded*. His work *Monument (If It Bleeds, It Leads)* is also cartography as anti-monument, but it doesn't so much create an alternative experience, or interstices of the marvellous in the present, as reproduce the perversion of desiring the "action" or "violence" recorded in the news or, on the other hand, the false tranquility of no action at all.

Manu Luksch's *The Faceless Project* (2002-7) treats CCTV footage as "legal readymades" – using images obtained under terms of the UK Data Protection Act, Luksch creates the movie *FACELESS* (2007) with the hidden/blacked out faces of persons whose privacy is protected when CCTV recordings are released. It is part of Luksch's "Manifesto for CCTV Filmmakers" that the film must include "activity of the protagonist" that "must qualify as personal or sensitive data… circumscribing the field of action for the actors relative to it, so that incidents of biographical relevance (i.e. that reveal personal data) occur in the frame."[24] Luksch's fable quite literally builds itself around restoring the "face" of its subject, an anxiety that runs throughout the exhibition in various forms. On one level Luksch broaches the "face" as the problematic crux of the "human," with all its resonance from Levinas' "proximity of the other" to Deleuze and Guattari's complex treatment of "faciality" as diagrammatic "pattern recognition."[25] On a more immediate one her effort is an aggressive attempt to "reclaim the data body."

How difficult that may prove to be is an at times unintended consequence of watching Peter Galison and Robb Moss' documentary *Secrecy* (2007) on the exponential expansion of government secrecy in the U.S. under the aegis of the "national security state." While putting into question the post-9/11 suspension of civil liberties and vast multiplication of classified information (including information, in some cases decades old, that was previously declassified!), Galison and Moss stay well within the limits of what passes for political discourse in the U.S., and so do not question terms like "national security" and "terrorism" themselves. An effective documentary, *Secrecy* plays on the human elements involved, including that of human error, only multiplied under such secrecy regimes.[26] The larger geopolitical context of why the U.S. spends twice as much as the rest of the world combined on "national security," is not brought into any focus. Instead, the issue of multiplied government secrecy is kept within a protocological problematic.

Tracing a similar genealogy in the UK, Rebecca Baron's documentary *How Little We Know of Our Neighbors* (2005) looks at the history of the Mass Observation Movement, a sort of "anthropology at home" entwined with the history of photography, of eavesdropping, of government surveillance, and ultimately mass marketing. The film traces observation from the invention of the instantaneous photograph, then the "detective" or hand camera, to the overlapping histories of eugenics, documentary film, taxonomies of all kinds, their imbrication with monitoring devices and marketing surveys, and wartime population control and espionage to the widespread CCTV surveillance of today. Themes of voyeurism and exhibitionism, joined invariably with any history of photography, make Barron's work a more accessible, if still innovative counterpart to Harun Farocki's intellectual cinema.[27] In Farocki's *Images of the World and the Inscription of War* (1988) this prolific, analytic experimental documentarist and artist takes bead on the instrumentalisation of vision, in which technoscientific, military, and political complexes combine with the technologies of film and photography to produce a nearly omnipresent world-picture.[28] Like the images of washing waves of the experimental wave pool that periodically crosses the screen, Farocki keeps bringing us back to the "blind spot" of such technological applications, most signally, the overlooking by evaluators of the Auschwitz concentration camp next to I.G. Farben industrial plant, taken by Allied pilots in 1944, and only realised by CIA analysts decades later.

Some of the wide range of critical strategies, appropriations, and genealogies featured in *Recoded* almost by necessity had to leak out of the gallery context and spill into the social life of the "street." Formed by intense investigation and conversation back and forth with the worlds of digital technologies and the social-political artifacts and shaping of daily life they so often create, works often slip into a "post-aesthetic" mode. To be fully present may mean going incognito, donning another mask, working in another discipline, "disappearing"oneself. It is increasingly true on the level of semiotic production generally, as activist critic Brian Holmes writes, that "the greatest symbolic innovations are taking place in self-organisation processes unfolding outside the artistic frame." Holmes argues "it is from the reference to such outside realms that the more concentrated, composed, and self-reflective works" have their meaning.[29] Yet it remains necessary, given the far wider and deeper instaurations and revolts likely to come, as Holmes urges, for practitioners of all sorts, at the critical moment, to "dissolve...into the vortex of a social movement."[30] And it is in moments such as those that the convergence of 'information art,' recontextualisation and updated *détournement* one finds in *Recoded* become a user's manual.

< Jay Murphy >

1 http://uk.news.yahoo.com/rtrs/20080608/tpl-uk britainsurveillance-81f3b62.html. [accessed June 8, 2008]. That it is a former Conservative PM like John Major who has weighed in heavily against the proposed 42 day detention law for "terrorist" suspects parallels developments in the U.S., where former Nixon speechwriter William Safire strongly attacked the Patriot Act in the editorial pages of *The New York Times*, while a large majority of (supposedly oppositional) Democrats voted for it.

2 Richard Ford, " 'Big Brother' database for phones and e-mails," *The Times* (May 20, 2008): 1-2.

3 Demetri Sevastopulo, "US tells visitors they must register in advance," *Financial Times* (June 3, 2008): 1.

4 Alexander R. Galloway and Eugene Thacker. *The Exploit*. Minneapolis; University of Minnesota Press, 2007. pp. 135-7.

5 Hakim Bey. TAZ: *the Temporary Autonomous Zone*. Brooklyn: Autonomedia, 1991.

6 Susan Buck-Morss. *Thinking Past Terror*. London/New York: Verso, 2003. pp. 70-1.

7 Ibid. p. 72.

8 Quoted in interview with filmmaker Jonas Mekas, 101 n. 4 (February 1998): 2-3. Also see Calvin Tompkins. *Duchamp: A Biography*. New ed. London/New York: Pimlico 1998.

9 Jean Genet. *The Declared Enemy: Texts and Interviews*. Trans. Jeff Fort. Stanford: Stanford University Press, 2004.

10 Naomi Klein. *The Shock Doctrine*. London/New York: Penguin Books, 2008. p. 303.

11 Ibid. Witness the extraordinary success of a consulting group like Giuliani Associates, although Mayor Rudolph Giuliani's multi-million dollar anti-terrorist command and control post in the World Trade Center completely vaporised on September 11.

12 Ibid. p. 302.

13 These wide chasms between the technological capacity to collect information and the bureaucratic inability to comprehend it, is a central theme of James Bamford's various books on the U.S. National Security Agency (NSA) and the U.K. Government Communications Headquarters (GCHQ), see James Bamford: *The Puzzle Palace*. London/New York: Penguin Books, 1983; *Body of Secrets*. New York/London: Arrow Books, 2002; *A Pretext for War*. New York: Doubleday, 2004; and the forthcoming *The Shadow Factory*. New York: Doubleday, 2008. For what some of these government and police surveillance centers look like and how they operate from the inside, see Matthew Brezezinski. *Fortress America*. New York: Bantam Books, 2005.

14 Naomi Klein, "Police State 2.0," *The Guardian*: G2 (June 3, 2008): 4-9.

15 Ibid. p. 7.

16 Gilles Deleuze. *Negotiations*. Trans. Martin Joughin. Minneapolis: University of Minnesota Press, 1990. p. 178. This is not to deny that even given the growing precedence of new forms of the "control" society, that multiple forms of what, according to Michel Foucault and Deleuze, was the previous incarnation of "disciplinary" society don't also proliferate – witness the massive growth of the prison-industrial complex in the U.S., that now incarcerates more of its population than any other country in the world, its revival of "chain gang" labour and the prevalent police violence in its cities. This is emphatically not a matter of widely increasing freedom on one level in order to consolidate control on a "higher," macro level, as is supposedly characteristic of "control" societies. As one could see during Free Trade Area of the Americas (FTAA) protests in November, 2003 in Miami, Florida, where police fired rubber bullets at unarmed demonstrators for most of an afternoon, old-style repression is alive and well. In this instance, however, it was far from successful – due to widespread popular resistance across the Americas, the FTAA was ultimately dead and buried.

17 Alexander R. Galloway. *Protocol*. Cambridge/London: MIT Press, 2004. p. 8.

18 Ibid. pp. 50-1.

19 Galloway and Thacker. *The Exploit*. pp. 135-6.

20 Comments by Galloway, at "Recoded: Landscapes and Politics of New Media" Conference, Aberdeen, Scotland, April 26, 2008. Galloway's uncritical acceptance of Fredric Jameson's periodization of stages of 'capitalism,' is not one of his stronger points. One could argue, as does Chalmers Johnson, that given the corporate/state symbiosis and predomination of only nominally 'private' companies like Halliburton and Bechtel, that the U.S. is not primarily a 'capitalist' power at all, but rather a form of "right-wing socialism." See Chalmers Johnson. *Sorrows of Empire*. London/New York: Verso, 2004.

21 Groups were more than essential, they were decisive in the formation of the various modernisms and avant-gardes of the 20th century, but the collectives of recent decades have a very different complexion. There is a spate of recent titles defining this, see Brian Holmes. *Unleashing the Collective Phantoms*. Brooklyn: Autonomedia, 2008; Blake Stimson and Gregory Sholette. Ed. Collectivism After Modernism. Minneapolis: University of Minnesota Press, 2007; Johanna Billing, Maria Lind, and Nilsson Lars, Ed. *Taking the Matter into Common Hands*. London: Black Dog Publishing, 2007; Claire Bishop, Ed. *Participation*. London: Whitechapel Art Gallery, 2006; and Grant Kester, Ed. *Conversation Pieces*. Berkeley: University of California Press, 2004.

22 Quotes from Jens Strandberg. *Power Point*. Glasgow: self-published [for Recoded], 2008. See also Strandberg's website: http://www.1200m.org/jens/powerpoint.html [accessed June 2008].

23 Mark LaVine. *Why They Don't Hate Us*. Oxford: One World Publishing, 2005. n. 160 p. 419. For a discussion of how to develop these lines of alliance between artists, activists, and academics, see Pierre Bourdieu's *Acts of Resistance* (Cambridge: Polity Press, 1998) and *Firing Back* (London/New York: Verso, 2003). A stellar example of such collaboration would be the work of Israeli architect Eyal Weizman, see his *Hollow Land: Israel's Architecture of Occupation*. London/New York: Verso, 2007.

24 See www.ambientTV.NET.

25 Emmanuel Levinas. *The Levinas Reader*. Ed. Séan Hand. New York: Routledge, 1989. p. 82; Gilles Deleuze and Félix Guattari. *A Thousand Plateaus*. Trans. Brian Massumi. Minneapolis: University of Minnesota Press, 1987. p. 170.

26 As was seen recently in the UK when data discs containing personal information for 25 million child benefit claimants with HM Revenue and Customs went missing. This revelation in November 2007 was followed by reports of further unencrypted personal details lost for 600,000 potential recruits for the Department of Defense, of 370,000 customers of the bank HSBC, and 3 million drivers registered with the Driving Standards Agency. See http://www.independent.co.uk/news/uk/home-news/alarming-public-sector-data-breaches-revealed-813321.html [accessed June 2008]. These foibles, which reportedly caused

PM Gordon Brown to kick over a Downing Street desk, pale
in comparison with that of Canadian national Maha Arar, or
various Afghan cab drivers, swept up for torture in different
secret prisons, because they had a similar name to a "terror
suspect," mistakes all the more possible due to massive
government/corporate datamining.

[27] For comparison of Farocki's work with the investigative and
political documentaries of Joris Ivens and Chris Marker, see
the catalog to the exhibition *net_condition*. Timothy Druckey
and Peter Weibel. Ed. *net_condition*. Cambridge/London: MIT
Press, 2001.

[28] A classic analysis of this remains Paul Virilio. *War and
Cinema*. Trans. Patrick Camillier. London/New York: Verso,
1989.

[29] Holmes. *Unleashing the Collective Phantoms*. p. 93.

[30] Ibid.

Alexander Egger

everybody get out of the pool - the zines series

Strategies for the times of apathy and
autism: Selective interventions infiltrating
institutionalized and hierarchic representative
aesthetics on behalf of a multidimensional critical
reflection of culture and consumerism.

A manic appropriation of the world. Monotone, fast
production (technical restrictions and limitations
counter the humming up poses of glossy printing
techniques). Focusing on the transient, volatile,
unemployable and sorted out, lost moments, errors
in transmitting, superimpositions, fragmentary
memories. Steadily feeding the hysteria of the
mass-medial channels and crossing the stagnation of
lulling programmes injecting transmittable simple
portions of irritating interferences of one's own
production. Acting intuitively like a virus, without
claiming authorship or hinting to the sender. The
presupposed security and appeal of fragile, sensible
and poetic imagery (putting aside aggressive
slogans, shocking effects or marketing penetration)
and the intimate experience of reading establish a
situation where the viewer uncovers the protection
and is receptive to the subversive radical potential
of the second view.

< Alexander Egger >

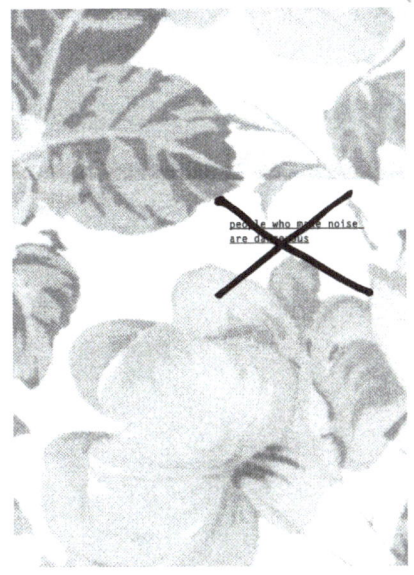

People who make noise
are dangerous

Copy/Paste as an established cultural
technique and working process to distribute
information in mass medial channels:
The identity as a form of differentiation between
subjects is veiled and partly dissolved through
repeated copying in favour of a fragile metalayer
which allows the singular images to merge and
furthermore to integrate into the surrounding world.
Accidental or deliberately lost or sorted out data
brought back in the focus of attention: Errors in
transmitting and editing lead to unexpected
results and open additional possibilities of
evaluation, omissions raise questions, frequent
copying eventually adds to the material a different
level of meaning not contained in the original:
A loss of detail and technologic quality is gained in
directness, raw power, grain, noise and texture.

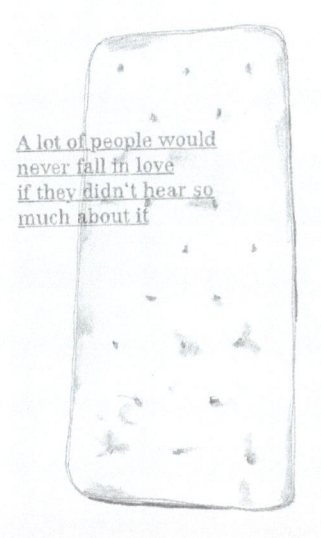

A lot of people would never fall in love
if they didn't hear so much about it

An experiment in influencing
the origination of personal memories: Deepening
and prolonging the intimate experience of sleeping
together in several beds through the act of drawing a series
of these sleeping situations with the aim to sensitize
one's senses to a more detailed and intensive
remembrance and anchoring in one's mind.
A naive longing for a conservation of transient
volatile feelings through fixing it in drawings.
A collaboration with Claudia Weissteiner.

Places to go, people to see,
things to do

Angst-driven and paralyzed in your
actions? What happens to you happens to
everybody. Everybody feels a little bit lost sometimes.
Introducing an unagitated simple activism in
daily life as a counterpart to the stagnation in
pseudo-individualistic myspace-profiles, the
morbid glamour of the appealing aesthetics of
failure, the sleepwakling consensus of passive
consumerism, the autism of an ego-optimizing
lifestyle, never paying what it is promising.
A plan of action, re-politicization of
microprocesses: Work, don't lament.

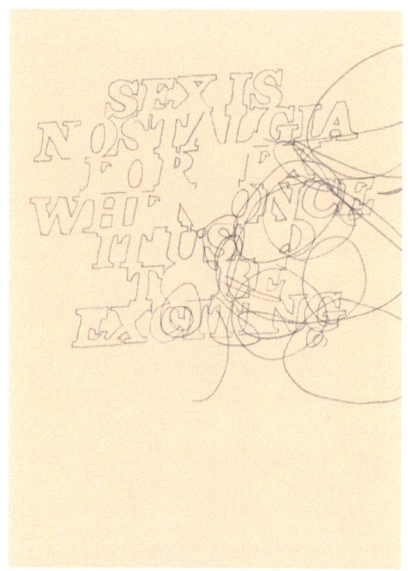

Sex is nostalgia for sex when once
it used to be exciting

The pressure and aggressive penetration
of sexual pleasure is present everywhere
and at any time and results consequently in over-
charged, isolated, sad and intimidated individuals:
Stories about serial consumption of sex, cheap
love, extended intimacy and the disappointment,
emptiness and sadness when everything
is revealed.
Drawings based on pictures sent via e-mail by
the users of an erotic chat during a logged-in period of 5 hours. The "revealing" formal, abstract
character of the drawings is able to bring back
the intimacy and mystery to the ostentativeness
of the basic material.

(The title is a citation by German writer Rainald Goetz)

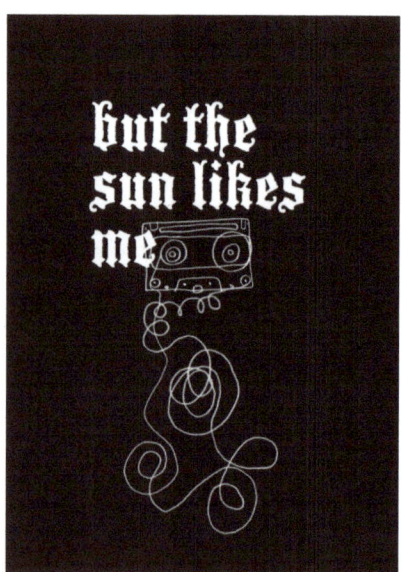

But the sun
likes me

Field studies analyzing the symbol
soup of everyday information in an accountan-
cy of existance: changing signs, easy marketing
targets, dying storage formats, broken cassette
mixtapes, bold headlines, repetitions, routines
and rituals, borrowed and stolen symbols, mis-
leading orientation systems and dark pleasures.
Recording, arranging, disentangling the amal-
gamation of grammars and codes of everyday
occurrences. Imparting personal reality through
description and classification in an arbitrary and
constructed system.

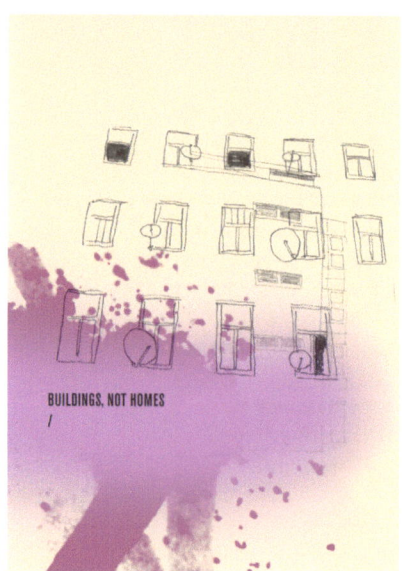

Buildings,
not homes

Interventions on urban structures:
Residential buildings, police helicopters,
representative avenues, shouted out loud slogans,
satellite dishes on the opposite side of the street,
demonstrations (of power), rank growth in public spaces, ambulance headlights, burning cars
and riots in Copenhagen, Paris, Budapest,
Belgrad...

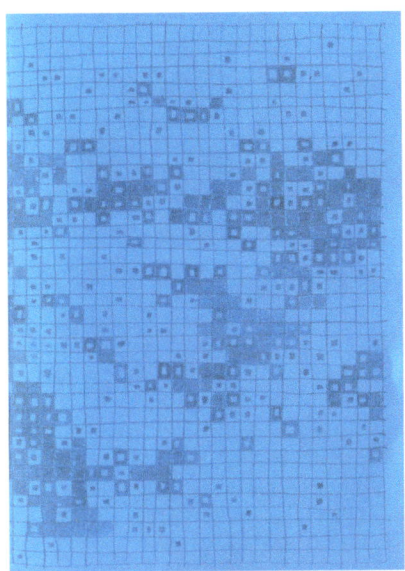

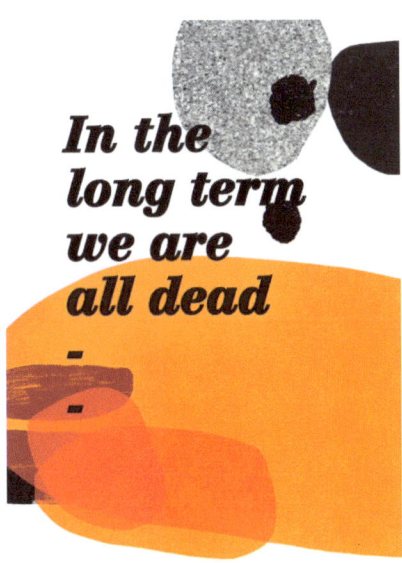

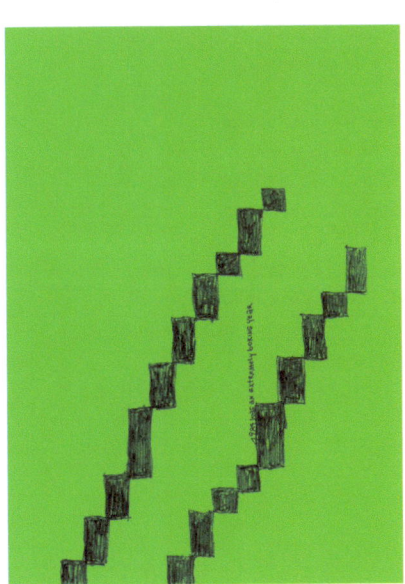

Weather
observations

Date: December 27, 2007.
Location: Milan/Italy. Current conditions:
Cloudy.

In the long term
we are all dead

The silent and cautious poetry of the
chants of the dead arising from the debris of
scorched lanscapes after the
apocalyptic decline: Notes and thoughts inspired
by a headline in an Austrian newspaper belon-
ging originally to an article about globalisation
and the devastating effects of the economic
theories of Milton Friedman.

Only a crisis – actual or perceived – produces
real change. When that crisis occurs, the actions
that are taken depend on the ideas that are lying
around. That, I believe, is our basic function: to develop
alternatives to existing policies, to keep them alive
and available until the politically impossible becomes
politically inevitable.
Milton Friedman, Capitalism and Freedom

1984 was an extremely
boring year

Retrofuturisme: Evaluating the actual situation
of the world according to George Orwell
and Martin Kippenberger in the year
1984. Minimal and abstract apocalyptic scenarios.
Generative hand drawn pixels re-demanding
production from the machines.

We're like bored children. We've been on holiday
for too long, and we've been given too many presents.
James Graham Ballard, Kingdom Come

text =
bad communication
-
connotation
machine
-
-
-

Irritation. How can you smile while you talk bullshit?

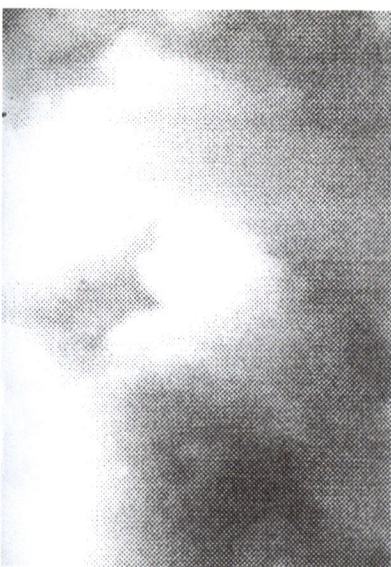

Text = bad
communication

Connotation machine.

Studies prove that the adressee doesn't get right
around 40 percent of the communication through
e-mails.

How can you smile while you
talk bullshit?

A questionnaire to develop a more
accurate self-assessment: Are you feeling old,
older than you really are and simultaneously
suffering from Peter Pan Syndrome and sucessfully
refusing to take responsibilities for yourself?

Look closely at the unidentified person in your
bathroom mirror. Move along. There's nothing
to see here. Questions result in a steep incline of
unanswered fragmentations. Gained knowledge
leads to the realization of an increasing amount
of agnosia. Ask the same questions again and
again, though. You never know if you have given
yourself enough time to get everything.

The top is just the bottom
in reverse

Every manifestation of a decision consists of
a process of selection and is a conscious blinding
out of all other aspects. As a consequence
everything presents itself containing infinite inherent
possibilities of other, different arbitrations. Everything
coeval contains also its opposite. Nothing is fixed,
everything is in a state of permanent flux.

Considering hope and confidence as a valuable
option in a unsafe and intangible world, it is
impossible to predict how one's personal biography
is developing. Not even death can be seen as
a definite end. With the passing of time some
estimations are possibly obsolete, prove themselves or have to be reviewed. Certain evaluations
are not even located in one's radius of action and
depending on external circumstances.

<Alexander Egger>

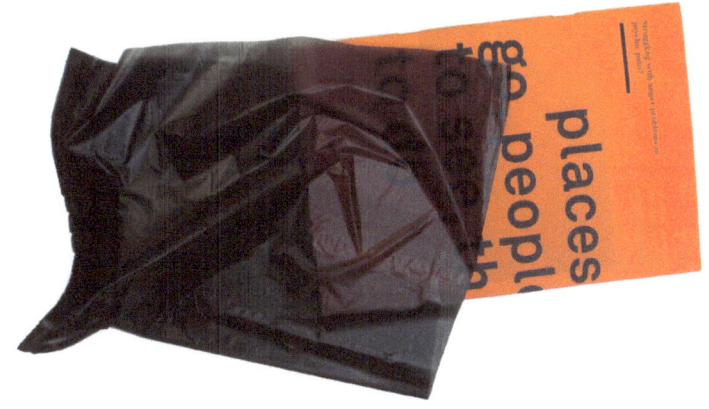

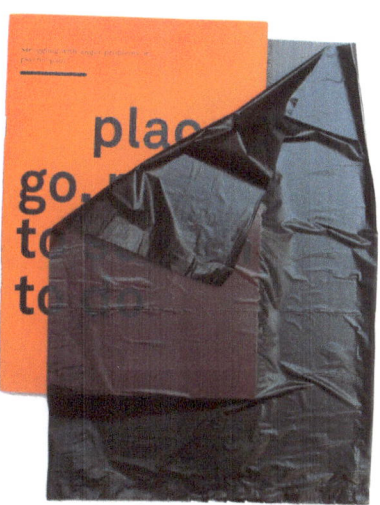

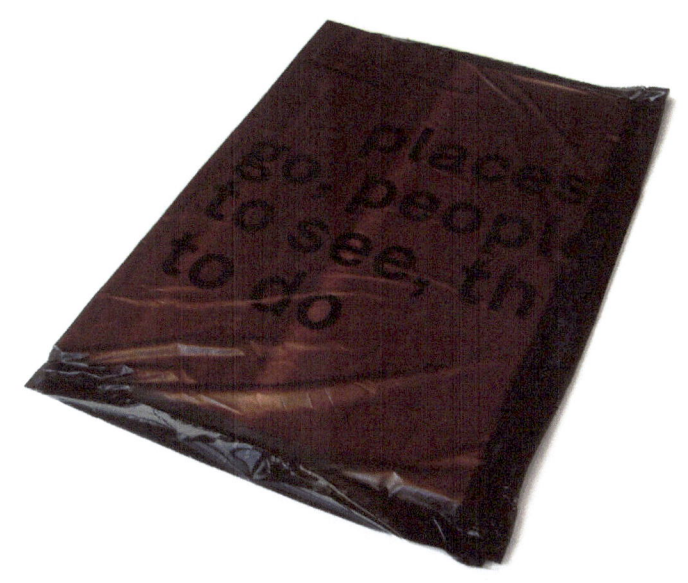

Places to go, people to see, things to do.

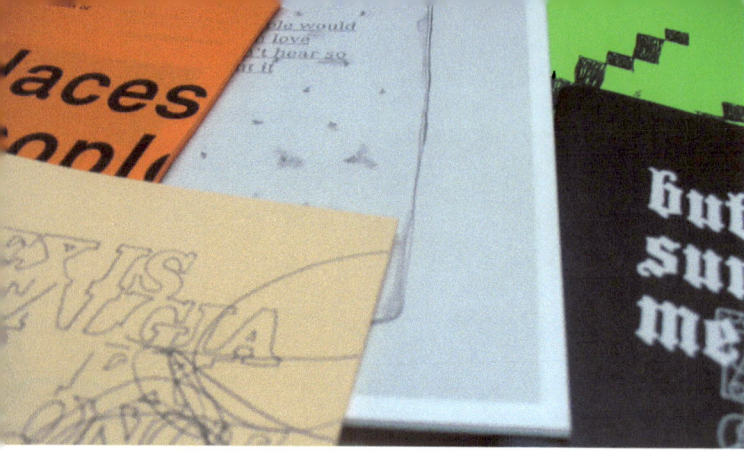

People who make noise are dangerous.

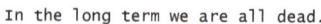

In the long term we are all dead.

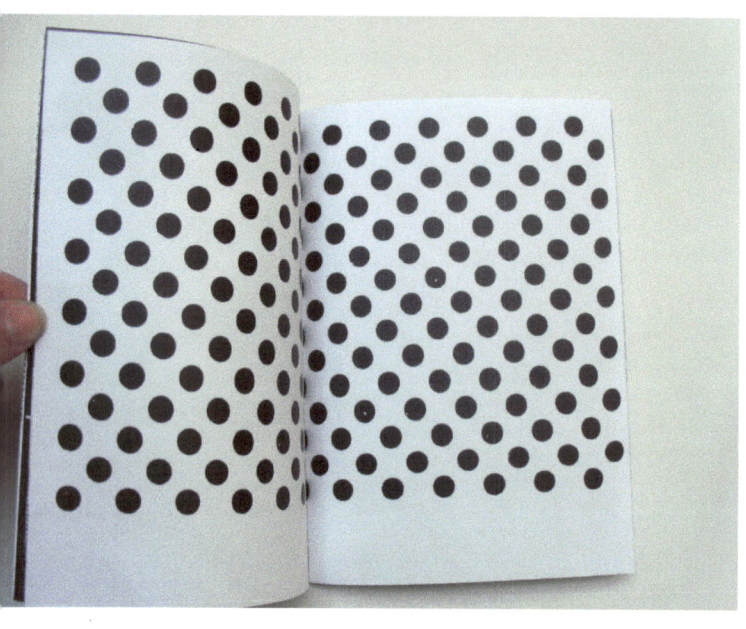

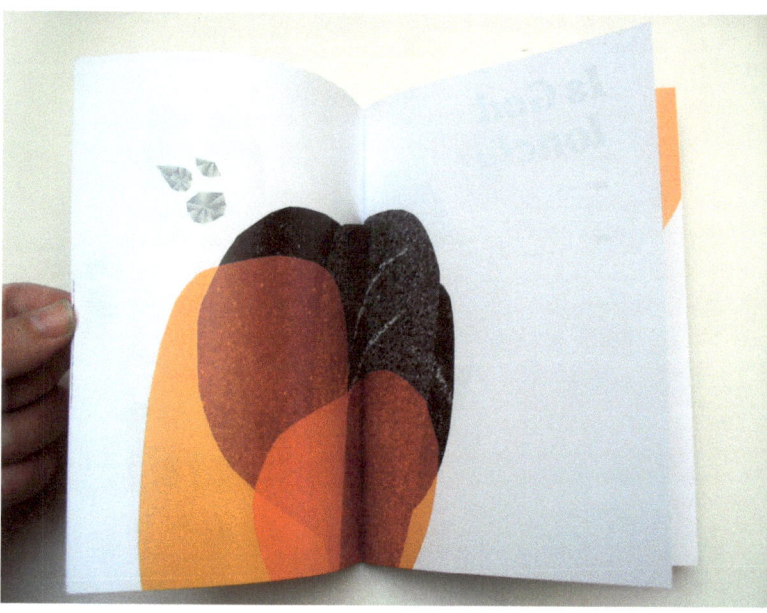

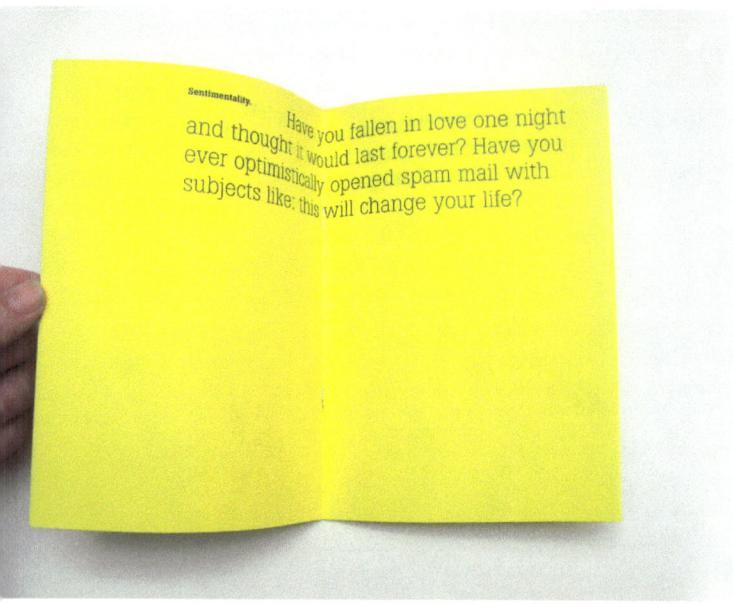

How can you smile while you talk bullshit?

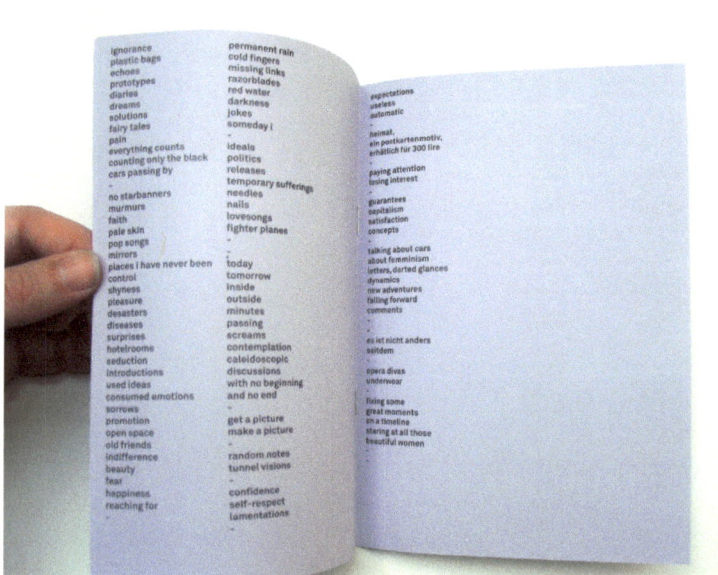

text = bad communication

Sex is nostalgia for sex when once it used to be exciting.

A lot of people would never fall in love if they didn't hear so much about it.

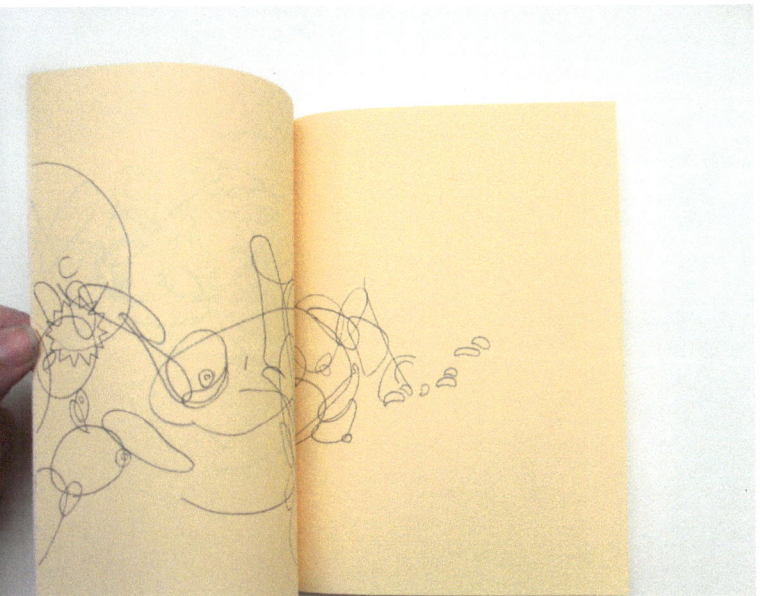

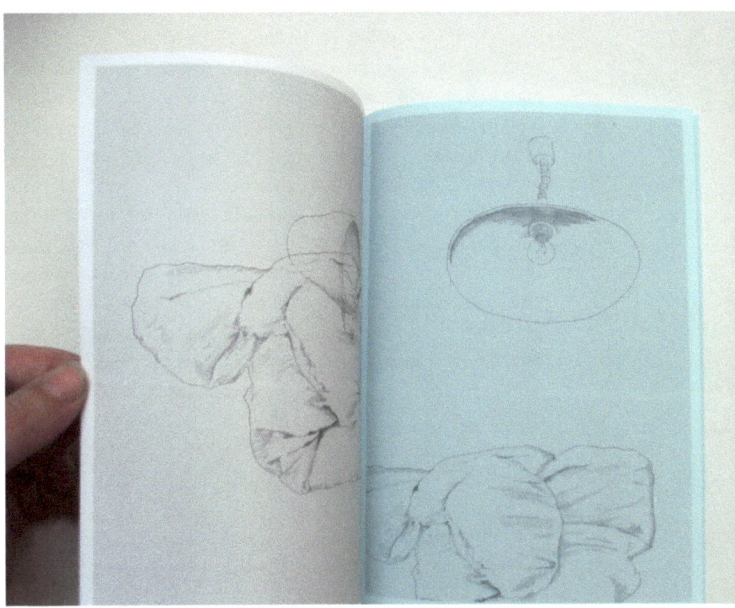

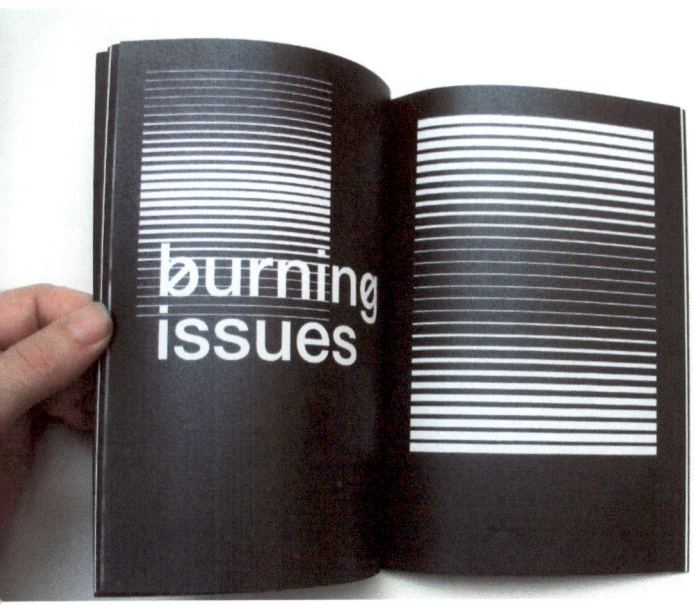

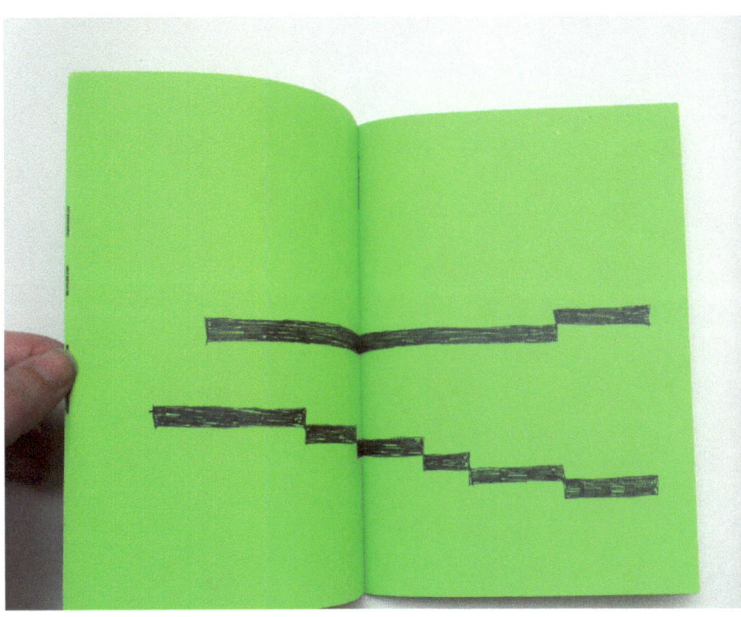

But the sun likes me.

1984 was an extremely boring year.

Anna Jermolaewa

Ass Peeping

"The fleeting glance, refuge of the anal"

Peep shows are a costly entertainment for voyeurs,
the lonely, tourists and stag nights. Hidden behind
the screen of a peep box and covered under the
protection of the night, the Peeping Toms risk
their greedy, furtive gazes onto the body which is
within reach, yet safely withdrawn. Anna Jermolaewa
turns this immutable institution on its head. She
is a voyeurist day walker, producing a dressed
peep show for a voyeuristic public. The backdrop
for Ass Peeping is the very busy shopping area
Mariahilferstraße in Vienna. The props are small,
fat, narrow, wide, long, old, young, pert and flabby
human behinds, moving forward in a mobile, sashaying
manner and thereby transforming the backdrop into
a cat walk. One after the other. Short or long
trousers, hotpants or shorts, minis, long skirts or
dresses - every model finds its place. Jermolaewa
manipulates the normal, lifts it out of its context
and renders it absurd. Through the naturalness of
the representation one's own expectations and those
of others recede into the distance. The work has a
lot of wit and irony, and reminds of the daily duel
between body and social environment.

< Judith Reichart, Bregenz, 2003 >

*)Peeping means voyeur in language usage, but it is also Michael
Powell's eponymous film from 1960.

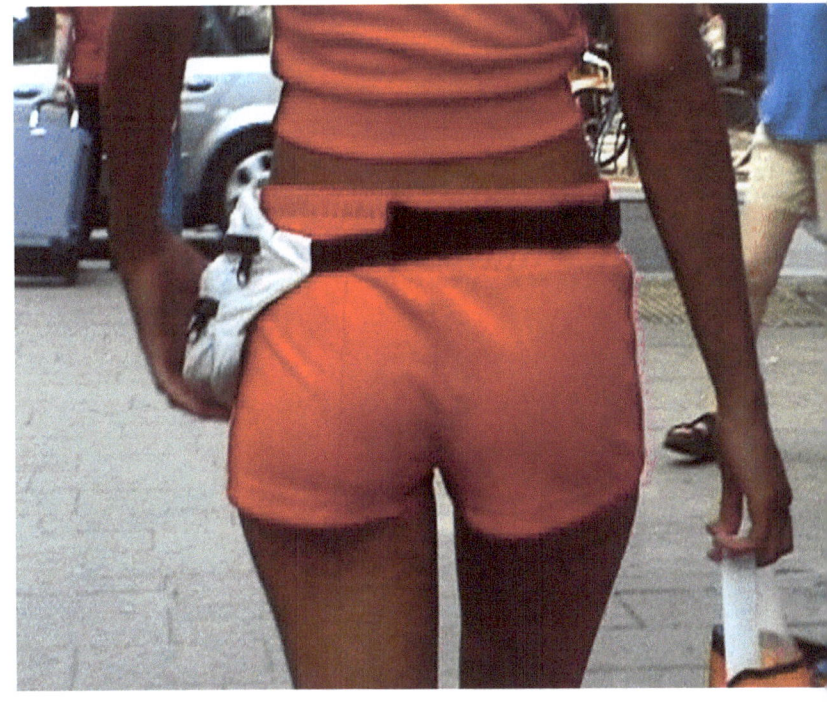

Ass Peeping, 2003
Stills from video

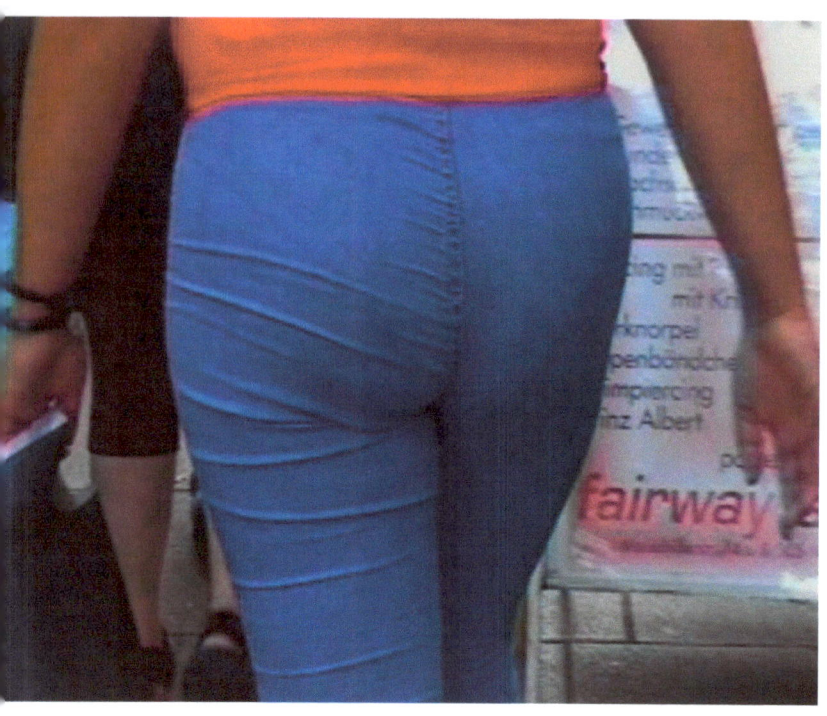

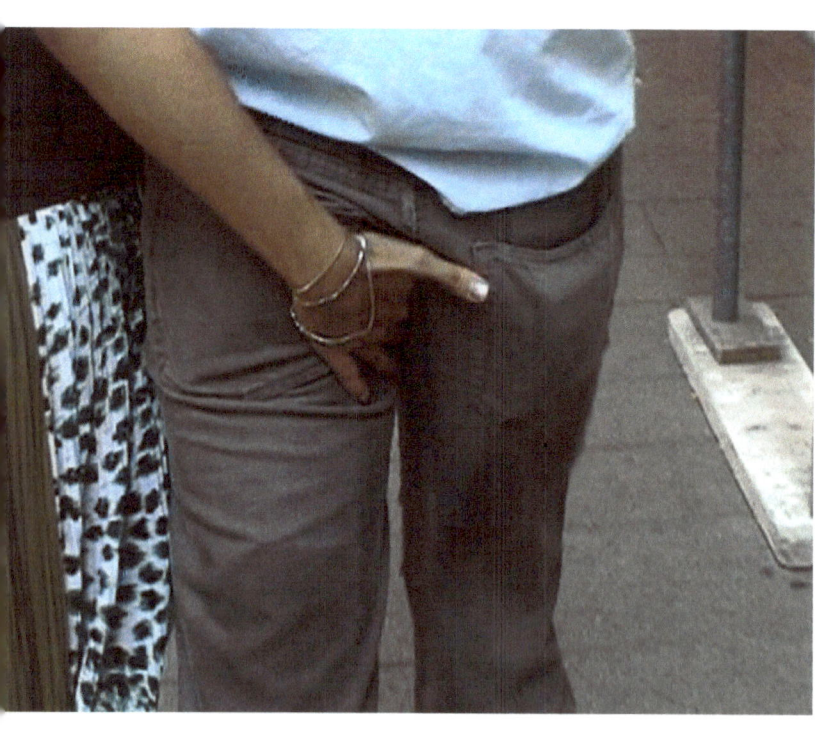

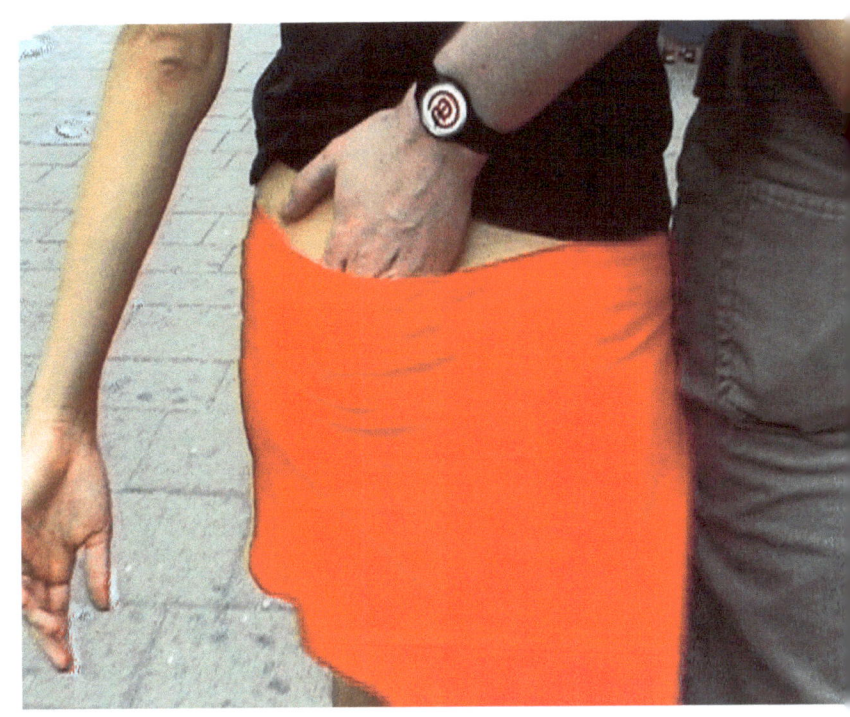

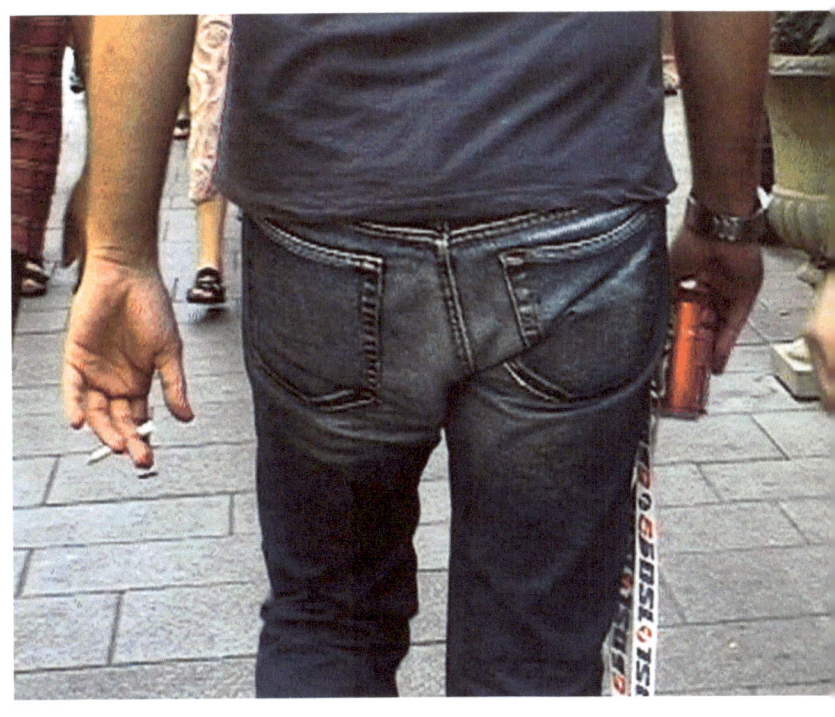

Caleb Larsen

Monument <if it Bleeds, it Leads>

Caleb Larsen's installation *Monument (if it Bleeds, it Leads)* (2006) continuously scans, via Google-News, the headlines of 4,500 English-language news sources around the world, looking for people who have been reported killed. For each death a ceiling-mounted mechanism drops a small yellow ball (a BB) into the room. During the course of the installation, BBs will accumulate on the floor, eventually covering it, with errant BBs traveling throughout the building. The contrast between the yellow balls rolling around and the puddle of blood they represent could not be bigger. While the BBs, used for combat games, normally symbolize the imitation of killing, here, in the context of art, they signify real killings. The subtitle puts it in dry, unmistakable words: *if it Bleeds, it Leads*. The BBs are contained in a transparent box containing 100,000 BBs, showing all of the balls not yet dropped and emphasizing the severity of the situation.

The dichotomy between the playfulness of the material and the sobering reality of the subject matter is, as Larsen states, clearly the intention of the work. This tension is combined with a confusing ethical situation since the viewer's natural inclination is to expect and desire activity from a kinetic sculpture: "the viewer finds himself secretly and selfishly waiting for someone to be killed only so that he can watch a little yellow ball bounce around on the floor." [1] Even the artist himself is entangled in this dilemma since his natural inclination is to verify the technical sophistication of his work while the implication of such proof compels him, rather, to wish his artwork does not happen. Monument challenges the technical narcissism that Marshall McLuhan describes as a human characteristic (see his essay *The Gadget Lover: Narcicuss as Narcosis*, in: Understanding Media, New York 1964) and that is so prominent in digital art and especially its genre of Mapping Art to which *Monument* belongs.

The tension between the playful ball and its deadly message aims right at the heart of contemporary media society and the society of the spectacle where news about catastrophes, riots, wars, and killings are a kind of entertaining element in our everyday life. The drop of the BBs is charged to an extent that one must wish the artwork would not reveal itself in action. Of course, the wish that nothing would happen does not prevent the next BB from falling. This experience is the message one has to bear: that (to reverse Jean-François Lyotard's notion of the sublime in postmodern art) something happens and not nothing. The audience may feel innocent; however, it can't be sure.

Monument not only undermines the sensory pleasure for its re-semanticization (or: détournement) of the BBs. It also challenges the cognitive pleasure that may occur because of the clever, compelling rendition of such a grim subject. The audience knows that it is the artist's aim to unsettle the audience by creating the tension described. The more the audience considers this undertaking successful, the more it will appreciate the artist's job. This equation creates the paradoxical situation that sensory discomfort turns into cognitive pleasure. In turn, becoming aware of this condition, one feels guilty for acquiring pleasure from the aestheticization of the horrible. Thus, this example of art finally elevates the tension between the playfulness of the material and its sobering meaning onto the higher level of aesthetic experience: as tension between the sobering reality and its artistic representation. The specific stylization of the information in *Monument* goes way beyond the mere presentation of data. It carries a symbolic depth that clearly makes the artist – his personal perspective, objection, and vision – visible in the piece.

< Roberto Simanowski >

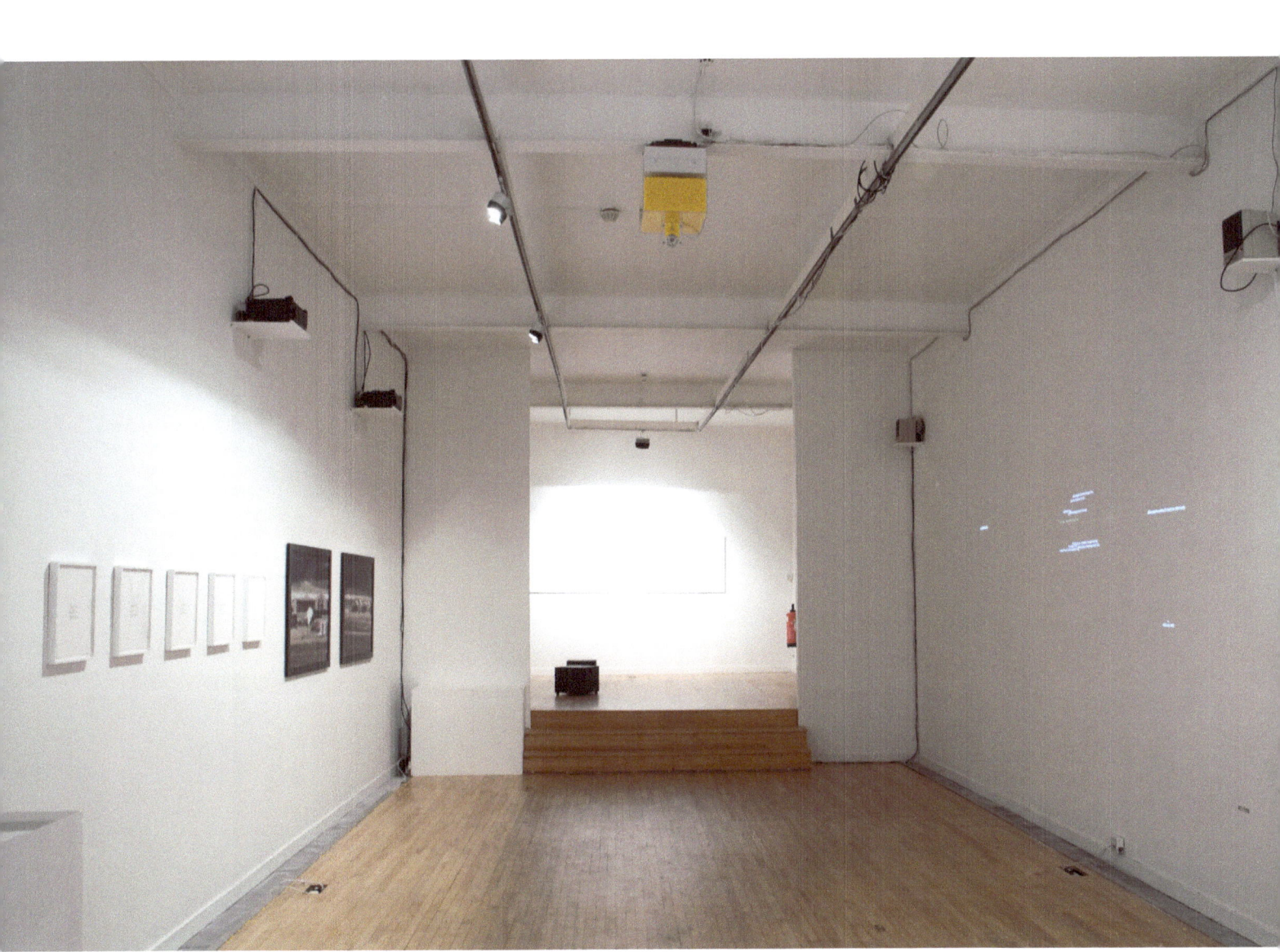

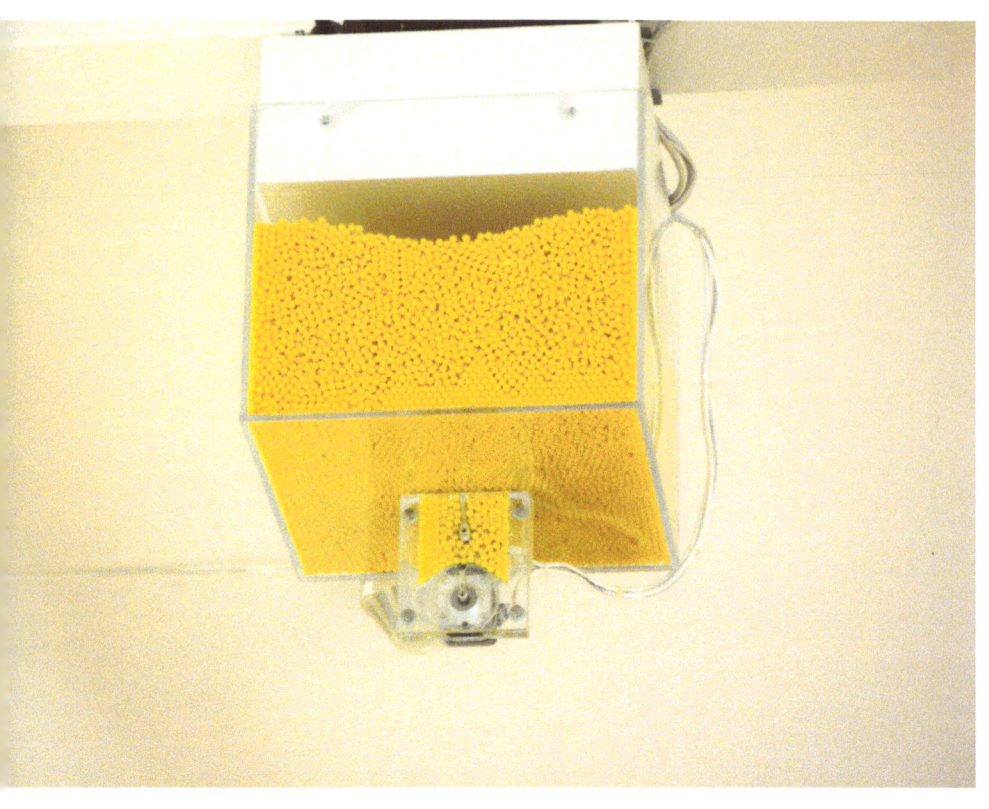

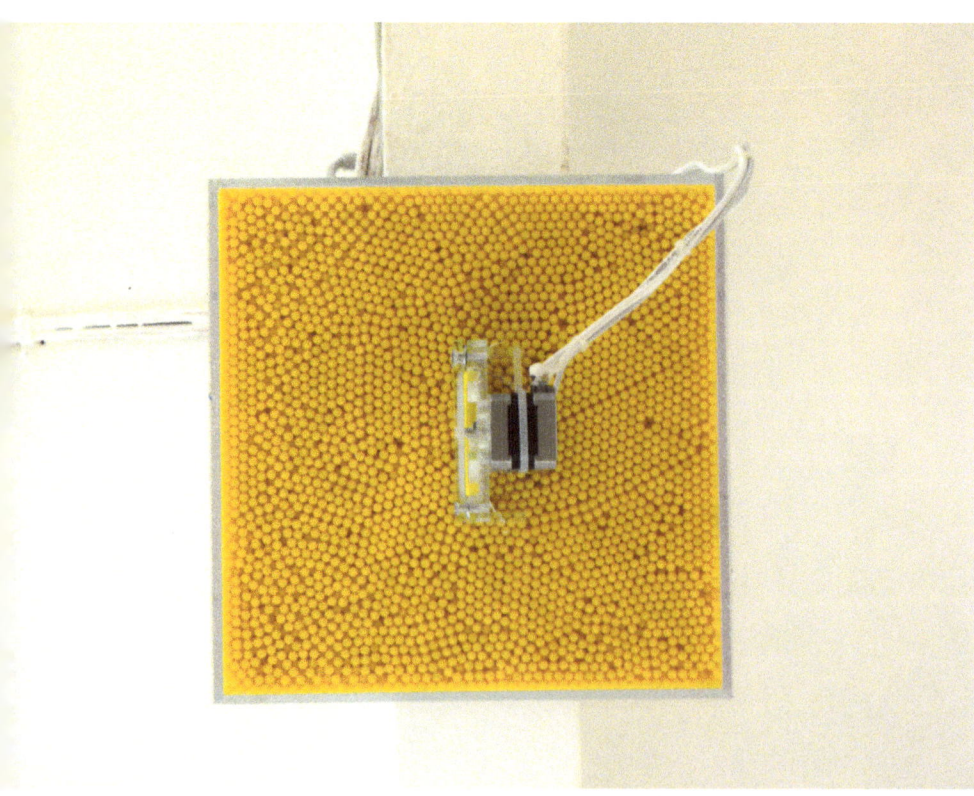

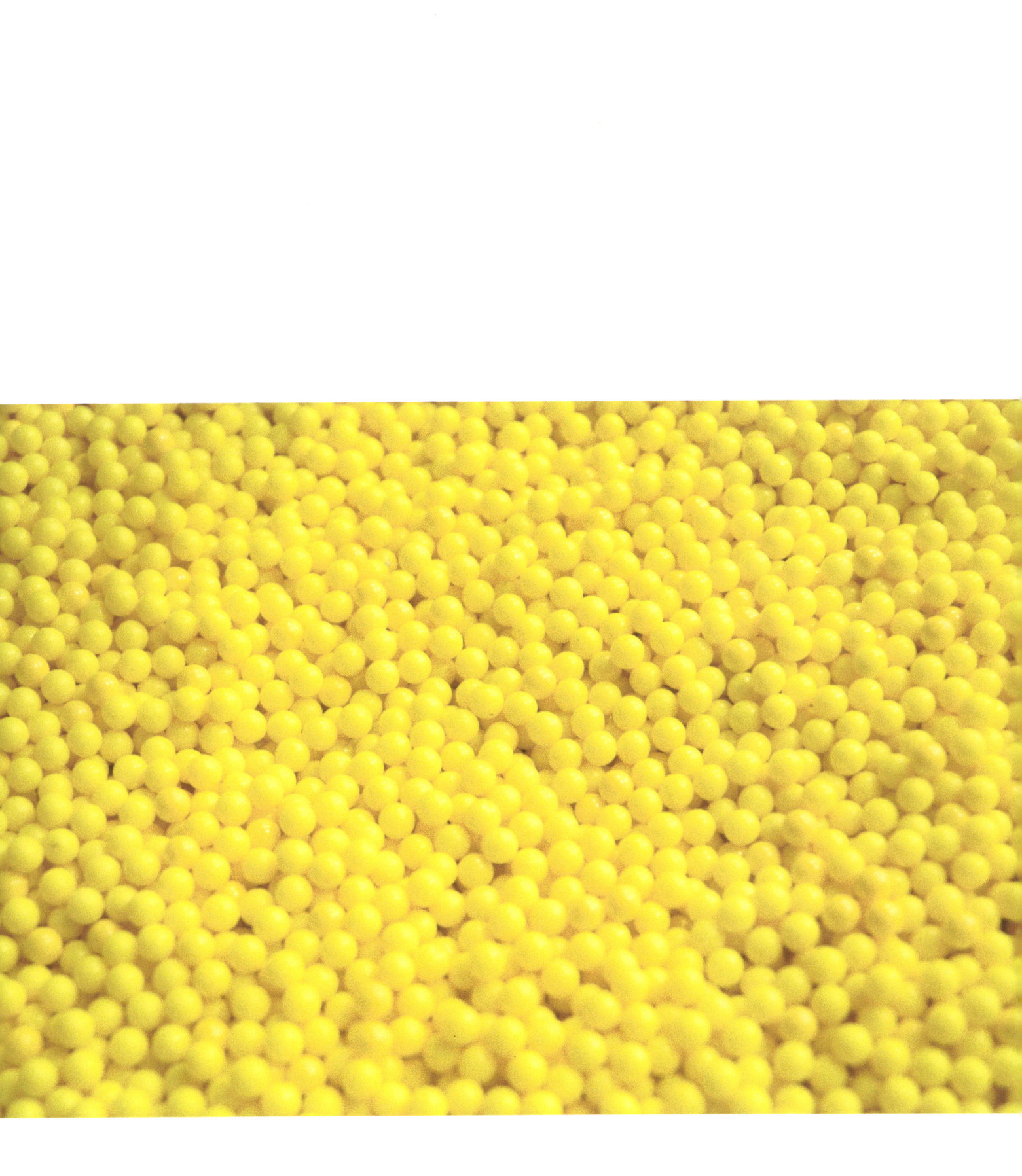

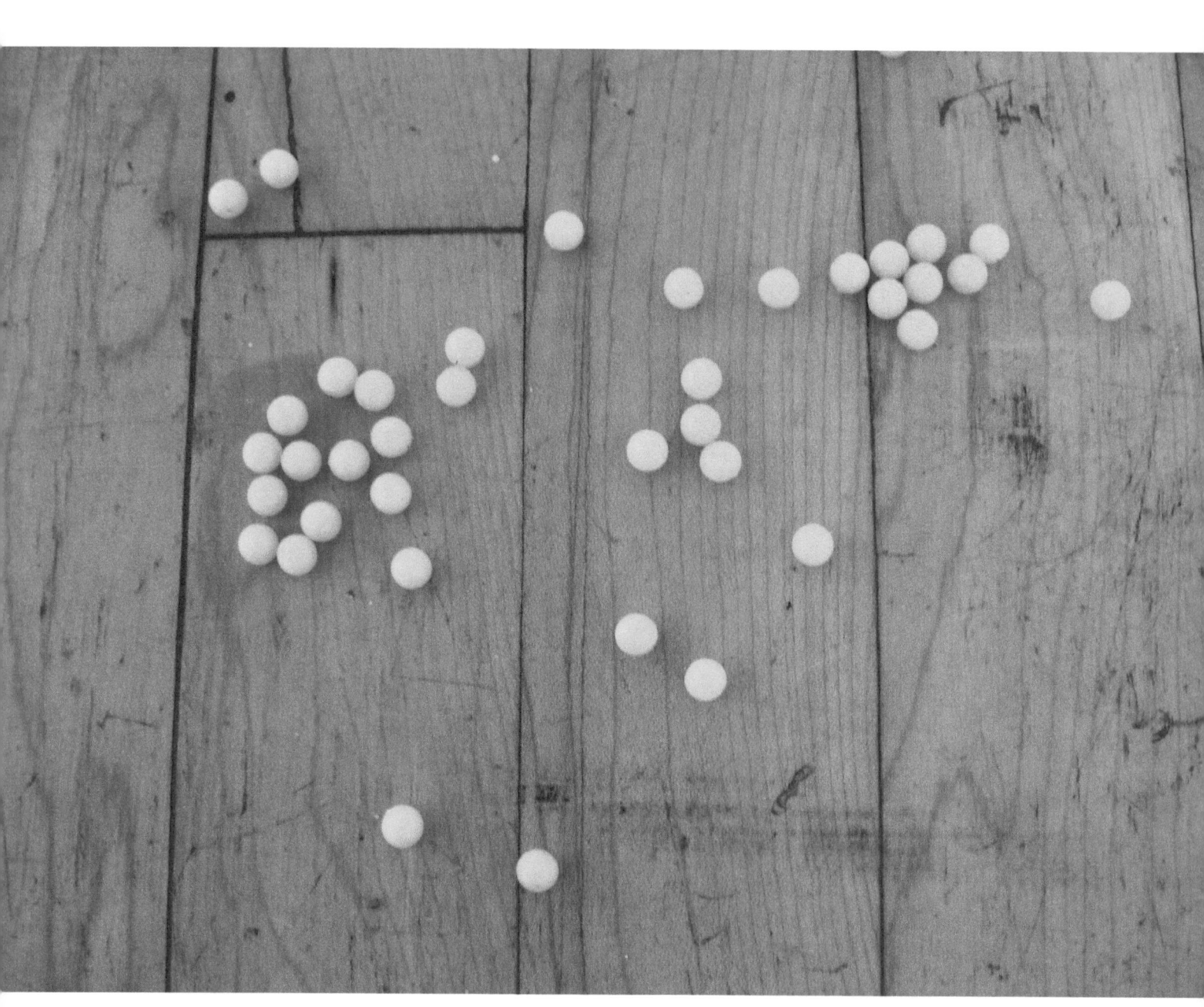

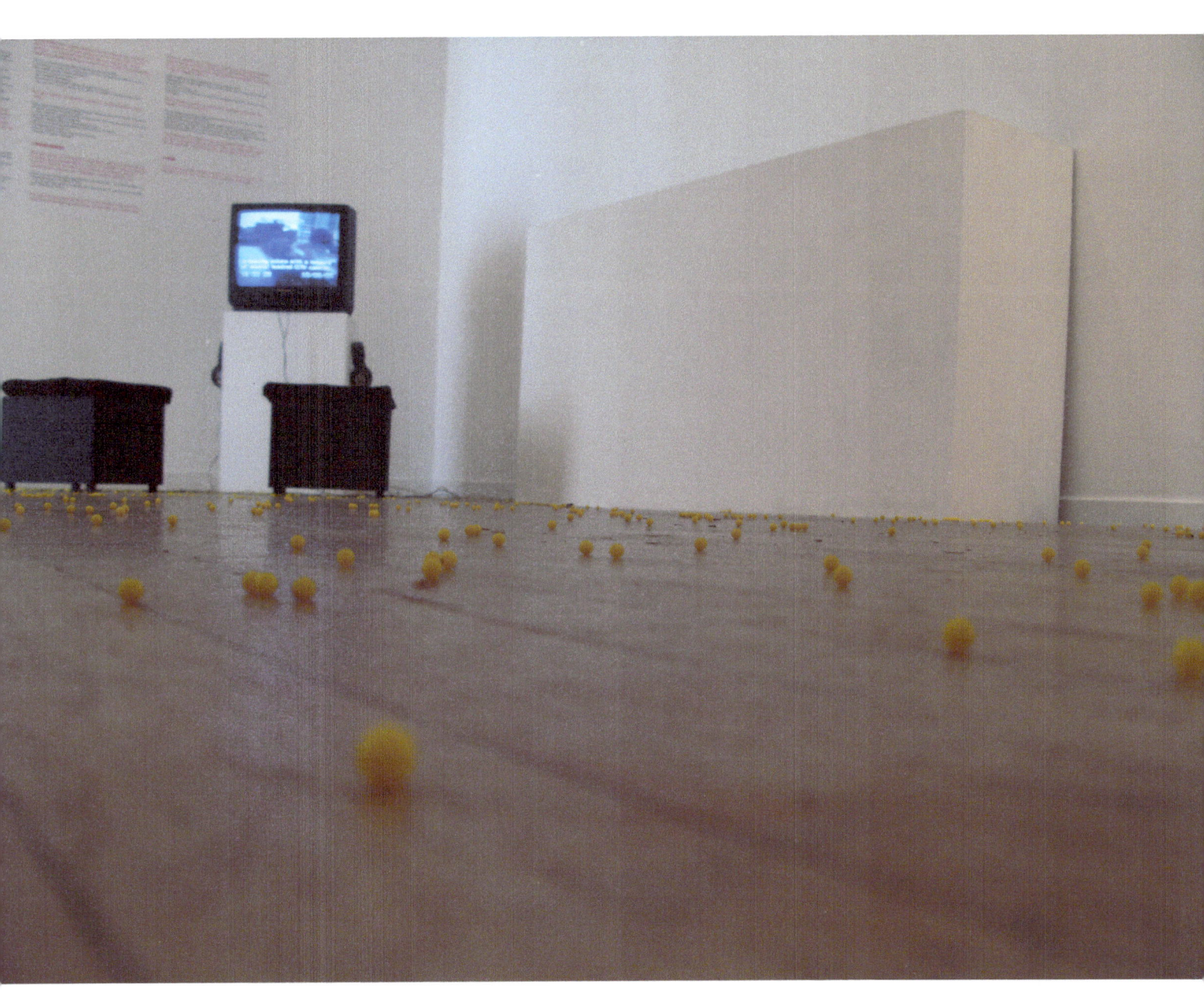

Manu Luksch

THE FACELESS PROJECT [2002-2007] dealt with the
legal attributes of CCTV images. The starting
point was the idea to produce a fiction film without
additional cameras, but by activating the legal
framework associated with the omnipresent video
surveillance.

FACELESS uses CCTV images obtained under the terms
of the UK Data Protection Act as 'legal readymades'.
Legislation requires that the privacy of other
persons be protected when data is released – for
CCTV recordings, this is typically done by obscuring
their faces – hence, the faceless world.

The process-led production of the film, FACELESS,
stretched over five years and resulted in a multitude
of works. A selection was shown in Recoded.

< Manu Luksch >

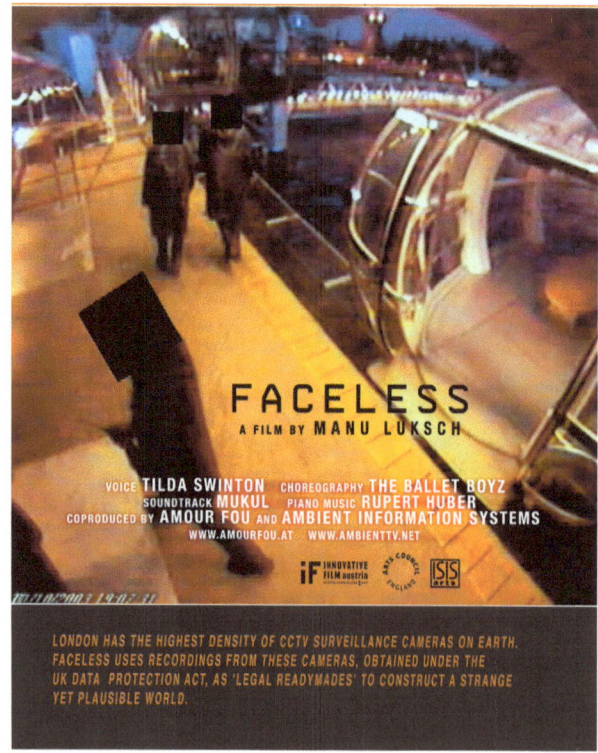

IN AN EERILY FAMILIAR CITY, A CALENDAR REFORM HAS DISPENSED WITH THE PAST
AND THE FUTURE, LEAVING CITIZENS FACELESS, WITHOUT MEMORY OR ANTICIPATION.
UNIMAGINABLE HAPPINESS ABOUNDS – UNTIL A WOMAN RECOVERS HER FACE ...

FACELESS
A FILM BY MANU LUKSCH

VOICE TILDA SWINTON   CHOREOGRAPHY THE BALLET BOYZ
SOUNDTRACK MUKUL   PIANO MUSIC RUPERT HUBER
COPRODUCED BY AMOUR FOU AND AMBIENT INFORMATION SYSTEMS
WWW.AMOURFOU.AT   WWW.AMBIENTTV.NET

iF INNOVATIVE FILM austria

LONDON HAS THE HIGHEST DENSITY OF CCTV SURVEILLANCE CAMERAS ON EARTH.
FACELESS USES RECORDINGS FROM THESE CAMERAS, OBTAINED UNDER THE
UK DATA PROTECTION ACT, AS 'LEGAL READYMADES' TO CONSTRUCT A STRANGE
YET PLAUSIBLE WORLD.

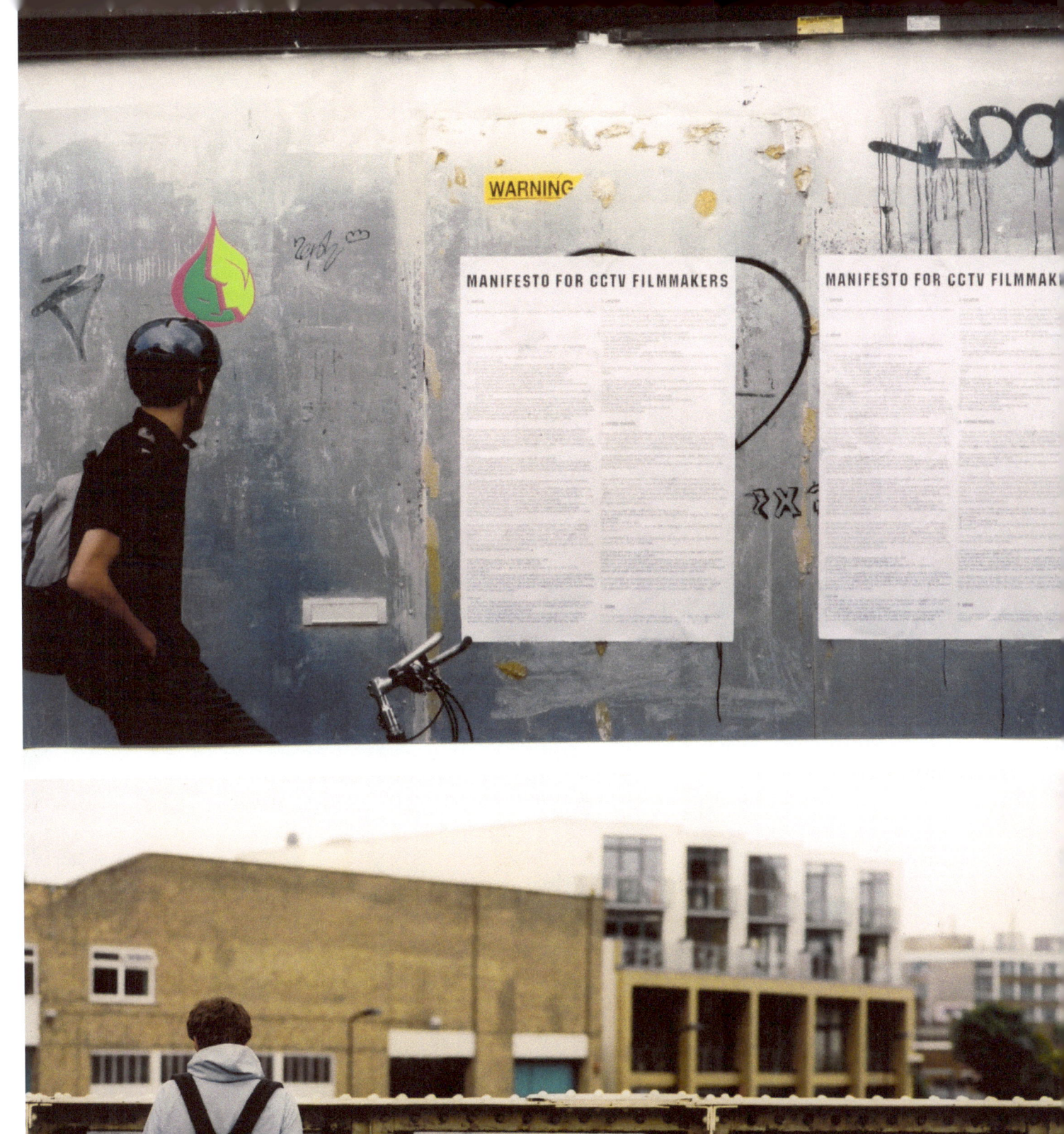

MANU LUKSCH
REGENT STUDIOS UNIT 76
8 ANDREWS ROAD
LONDON E8 4QN

28 August 2003

The security and safety manager,
Barclays Head Office
54 Lombard Street,
London EC3P 3AH

Dear Sir / Madam,

I wish to apply, under the Data Protection Act, for any and all CCTV images of my person held within your system. On 27 August 2003, I was present at the ATM 254 Seven Sisters Road, at approx. 20.15 p. m.

For ease of identification, I enclose a photo of myself below. I was wearing white trousers and a white T-Shirt with aqua blue sleeves.

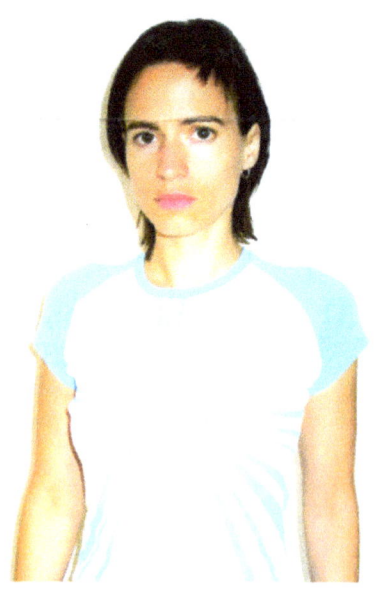

Reclaiming the data body

Through putting the DPA into practice and observing the consequences over a long exposure, close-up, subtle developments of the law were made visible and its strengths and lacunae revealed.

"I can confirm there are no such recordings of yourself from that date, our recording system was not working at that time." (11/2003)

Many data requests had negative outcomes because either the surveillance camera, or the recorder, or the entire CCTV system in question was not operational. In some instances, the non-functionality of the system was only revealed to its operators when a subject access request was made. In the case below, the CCTV system had been installed two years prior to the request.

"Upon receipt of your letter [...] enclosing the required £10 fee, I have been sourcing a company who would edit these tapes to preserve the privacy of other individuals who had not consented to disclosure. [...] I was informed [...] that all tapes on site were blank. [.. W]hen the engineer was called he confirmed that the machine had not been working since its installation.
Unfortunately there is nothing further that can be done regarding the tapes, and I can only apologise for all the inconvenience you have been caused." (11/2003)

Technical failures on this scale were common. Gross human errors were also readily admitted to:

"As I had advised you in my previous letter, a request was made to remove the tape and for it not to be destroyed. Unhappily this request was not carried out and the tape was wiped according with the standard tape retention policy employed by [deleted]. Please accept my apologies for this and assurance that steps have been taken to ensure a similar mistake does not happen again." (10/2003)

Some responses, such as the following, were just mysterious (data request made after spending an hour below several cameras installed in a train carriage).

"We have carried out a careful review of all relevant tapes and we confirm that we have no images of you in our control." (06/2005)

Could such a denial simply be an excuse not to comply with the costly demands of the DPA? Many older cameras deliver image quality so poor that faces are unrecognisable. In such cases the operator fails in the obligation to run CCTV for the declared purposes.

"You will note that yourself and a colleague's faces look quite indistinct in the tape, but the picture you sent to us shows you wearing a similar fur coat, and our main identification had been made through this and your description of the location." (07/2002)

To release data on the basis of such weak identification compounds the failure.

Much confusion is caused by the obligation to protect the privacy of third parties in the images. Several data controllers claimed that this relieved them of their duty to release images:

"[... W]e are not able to supply you with the images you requested because to do so would involve disclosure of information and images relating to other persons who can be identified from the tape and we are not in a position to obtain their consent to disclosure of the images. Further, it is simply not possible for us to eradicate the other images. I would refer you to section 7 of the Data Protection Act 1998 and in particular Section 7 (4)." (11/2003)

Even though the section referred to states that it is:

"not to be construed as excusing a data controller from communicating so much of the information sought by the request as can be communicated without disclosing the identity of the other individual concerned, whether by the omission of names or other identifying particulars or otherwise."

Where video is concerned, anonymisation of third parties is an expensive, labour-intensive procedure – one common technique is to occlude each head with a black oval. Data controllers may only charge the statutory maximum of £10 per request, though not all seemed to be aware of this:

"It was our understanding that a charge for production of the tape should be borne by the person making the enquiry, of course we will now be checking into that for clarification. Meanwhile please accept the enclosed video tape with compliments of [deleted], with no charge to yourself." (07/2002)

Visually provocative and symbolically charged as the occluded heads are, they do not necessarily guarantee anonymity. The erasure of a face may be insufficient if the third party is known to the person requesting images. Only one data controller undeniably (and elegantly) met the demands of third party privacy, by masking everything but the data subject, who was framed in a keyhole. (This was an uncommented second offering; the first tape sent was unprocessed.) One CCTV operator discovered a useful loophole in the DPA:

"I should point out that we reserve the right, in accordance with Section 8(2) of the Data Protection Act, not to provide you with copies of the information requested if to do so would take disproportionate effort." (12/2004)

What counts as disproportionate effort ? The gold standard was set by an institution whose approach was almost baroque – they delivered hard copies of each of the several hundred relevant frames from the timelapse camera, with third parties heads cut out, apparently with nail scissors.

Two documents had (accidentally?) slipped in between the printouts – one a letter from a junior employee tendering her resignation (was it connected with the beheading job?), and the other an ironic memo:

"And the good news – I enclose the £10 fee to be passed to the branch sundry income account." (Head of Security, internal communication 09/2003)

From 2004, the process of obtaining images became much more difficult.

"It is clear from your letter that you are aware of the provisions of the Data Protection Act and that being the case I am sure you are aware of the principles in the recent Court of Appeal decision in the case of Durant vs. Financial Services Authority. It is my view that the footage you have requested is not personal data and therefore [deleted] will not be releasing to you the footage which you have requested." (12/2004)

Under Common Law, judgements set precedents. The decision in the case Durant vs. Financial Service Authority (2003) redefined personal data ; since then, simply featuring in raw video data does not give a data subject the right to obtain copies of the recording. Only if something of a biographical nature is revealed does the subject retain the right.

"Having considered the matter carefully,we do not believe that the information we hold has the necessary relevance or proximity to you. Accordingly we do not believe that we are obligated to provide you with a copy pursuant to the Data Protection Act 1988. In particular, we would remark that the video is not biographical of you in any significant way." (11/2004)

Further, with the introduction of cameras that pan and zoom, being filmed as part of a crowd by a static camera is no longer grounds for a data request, or so some believe.

"[T]he Information Commissioners office have indicated that this would not constitute your personal data as the system has been set up to monitor the area and not one individual." (09/2005)

As awareness of the importance of data rights grows, so the actual provision of those rights diminishes:

"I draw your attention to CCTV systems and the Data Protection Act 1998 (DPA) Guidance Note on when the Act applies. Under the guidance notes our CCTV system is no longer covered by the DPA [because] we:
" only have a couple of cameras cannot move them remotely just record on video whatever the cameras pick up only give the recorded images to the police to investigate an incident on our premises" (05/2004)

Data retention periods (which data controllers define themselves) also constitute a hazard to the CCTV filmmaker:

"Thank you for your letter dated 9 November addressed to our Newcastle store, who have passed it to me for reply. Unfortunately, your letter was delayed in the post to me and only received this week. [...] There was nothing on the tapes that you requested that caused the store to retain the tape beyond the normal retention period and therefore CCTV footage from 28 October and 2 November is no longer available." (12/2004)

Amidst this sorry litany of malfunctioning equipment, erased tapes, lost letters and sheer evasiveness, one CCTV operator did produce reasonable justification for not being able to deliver images:

"We are not in a position to advise whether or not we collected any images of you at [deleted]. The tapes for the requested period at [deleted] had been passed to the police before your request was received in order to assist their investigations into various activities at [deleted] during the carnival." (10/2003)

< in: "Chasing the Data Shadow. Manu Luksch, Mukul Patel, in: Goodbye Privacy ed. Schöpf/Stocker 2007 >

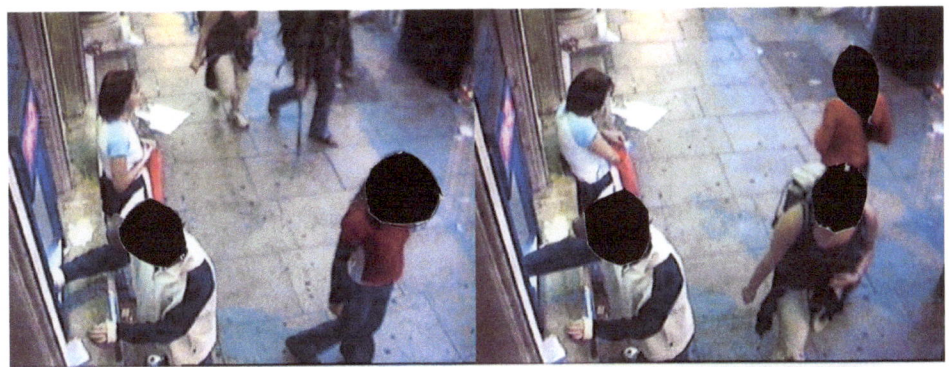

FINSBURY PARK N4 2HZ 20/46/57 - 6 (715)   FINSBURY PARK N4 2HZ 20/46/57 - 6 (537)
Camera - EXTERNAL ATM 1   Camera - EXTERNAL ATM 1
27/08/2003, 20:19:35:86   27/08/2003, 20:19:37:94
Digital Video Storage System   Digital Video Storage System
Camera -   Camera -
27/08/2003, 20:19:35:86   27/08/2003, 20:19:37:94

How to anonymise
Set of A4 documents, 2003
Original documents provided by a data controller in compliance withthe Data Protection Act (1998)
showing stills of CCTV recordings and the heads of third parties in the image cut out with scissors.

"I wish to apply, under the Data Protection Act, for any and all CCTV images of my person
held within your system. I was present at [place] from approximately [time] onwards on [date]."
Mixed media 150 cm x 37 cm, wood, neon light, transparencies. 2007

Excerpts taken from letters written by CCTV operators in response to subject data requests
but failing to comply. The title of the piece is taken from the artists' standard request letter.

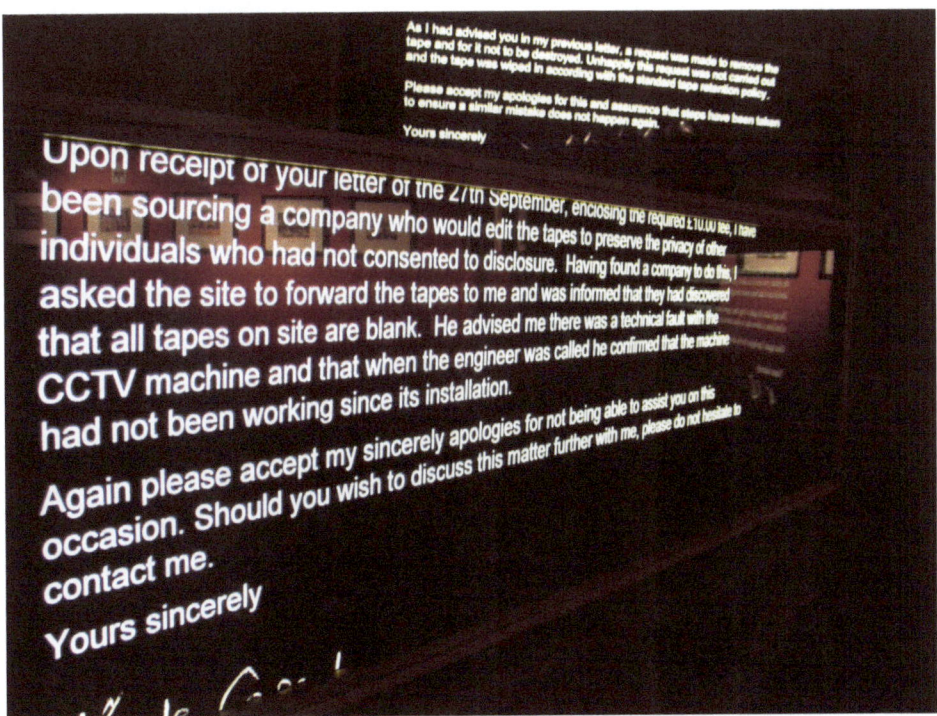

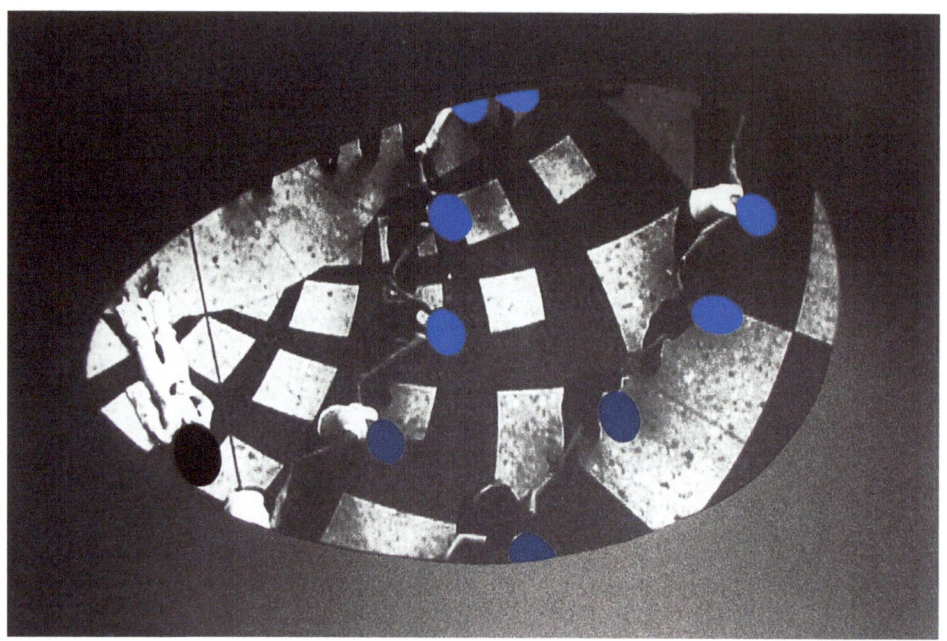

The Eye: Choreography for surveilled space, 2005
Two site-specific dance pieces choreographed for elevated point of view.

George Piper Dances (The Ballet Boyz) and Alluminae Dance Project
in collaboration with Manu Luksch created a site-specific dance piece for 80 performers,
developed as a humourous homage to the Busby Berkeley Hollywood revue movies.
The choreography unfolds like a kaleidoscope to be filmed from above - this time by means of CCTV.

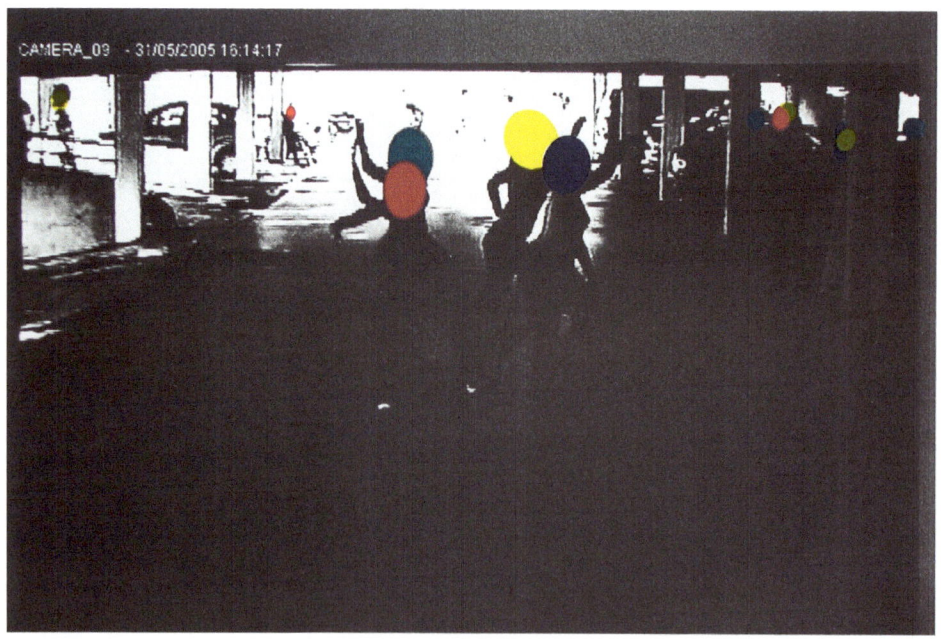

The sequences feature in FACELESS the movie and provided the images for the photographic
screen-prints of same name, printed with Linsay Croall at Peacock Visual Arts
(36 x 48 cm, edition of 12, 2008).

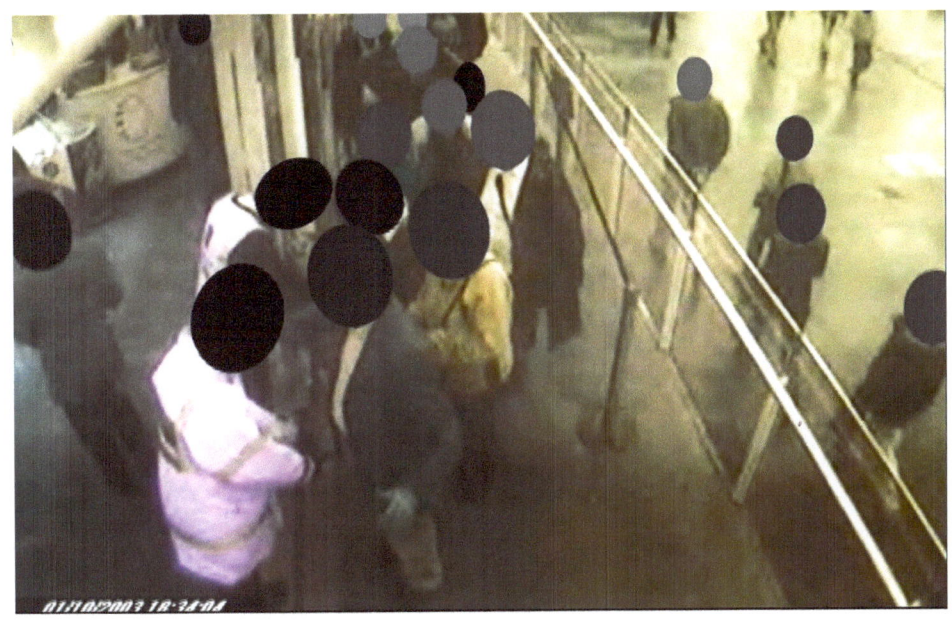

f00050102
Still of the film FACELESS (2007)

In a distant era, people had become discontented. Anxiety about the future and guilt over the past caused great unhappiness. The present was continuously in short supply. Then, a reform of the calendar was proposed to dispense with the troublesome past and future, and fill everyone's lives with the perfect present.

f00225518
Still of the film FACELESS (2007)

Circles whirl within circles, dreams within dreams. Maps, codes, rituals – the dance sings of many things strange to her. The movements articulate the circles of the letter, revealing hidden passages through the city.

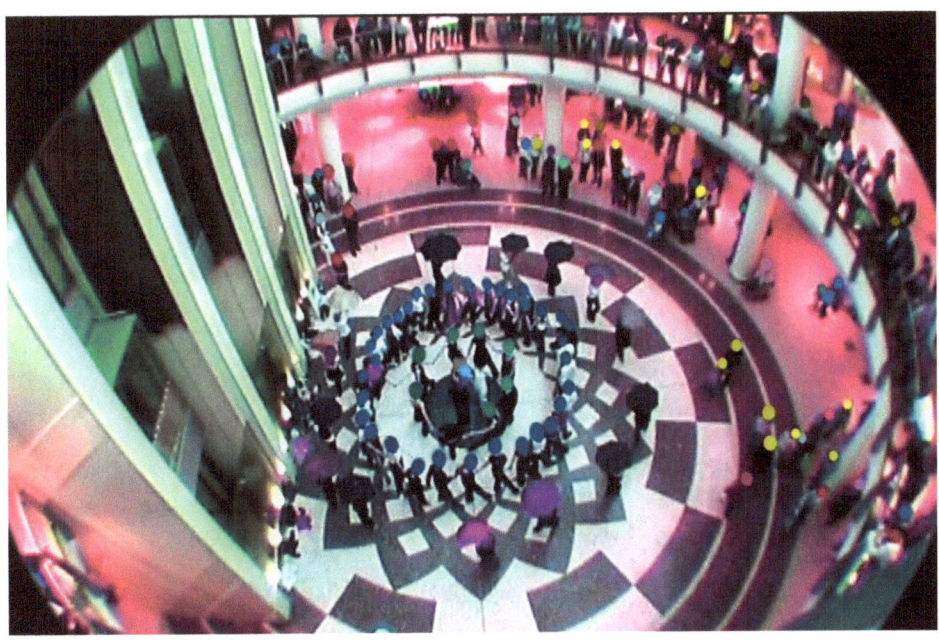

David Valentine / MediaShed

The Duellists

Free-running meets free-media film when two late
night traceurs are caught on CCTV as they engage in
an acrobatic competition in the Manchester Arndale
shopping centre. Filmed using only the in-house
CCTV network with a soundtrack created from the
environmental noises recorded during production.
Free-running uses uninterrupted movement adapting
motion to obstacles in the environment while
free-media film adapts environmental and discarded
hardware making filmmaking more accessible to all.

For Futuresonic 2007, MediaShed were invited to
create a piece for the exhibition Art for Shopping
Centres. Filmmaker David Valentine worked with
professional parkour breakin' crew Methods of
Movement to choreograph and shoot a short film over
three consecutive nights, using only the existing
in-house CCTV network of 160 cameras operated
from the central control room. Electronic artist
Hybernation composed the soundtrack from the found
sounds he recorded while the film was being made.

The project represents the first official UK
implementation of Gearbox: the free-media video
toolkit developed by MediaShed with the Eyebeam
Studios in New York, as part of Eyebeam's 2006/07
commissions program.

< MediaShed >

The Duellists, 2007
Stills from video

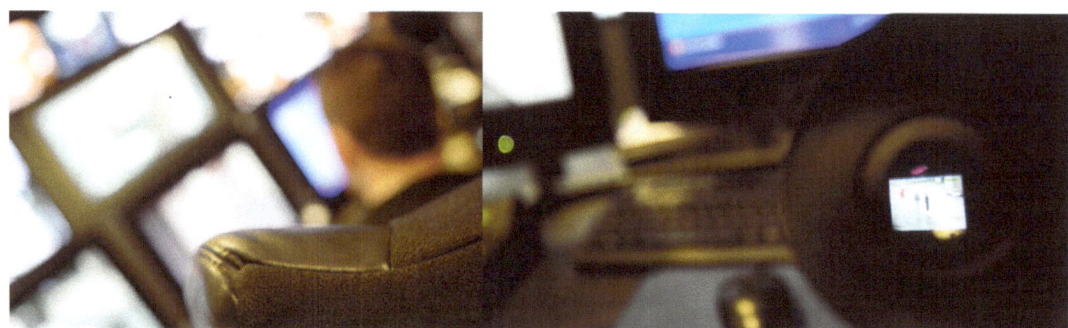

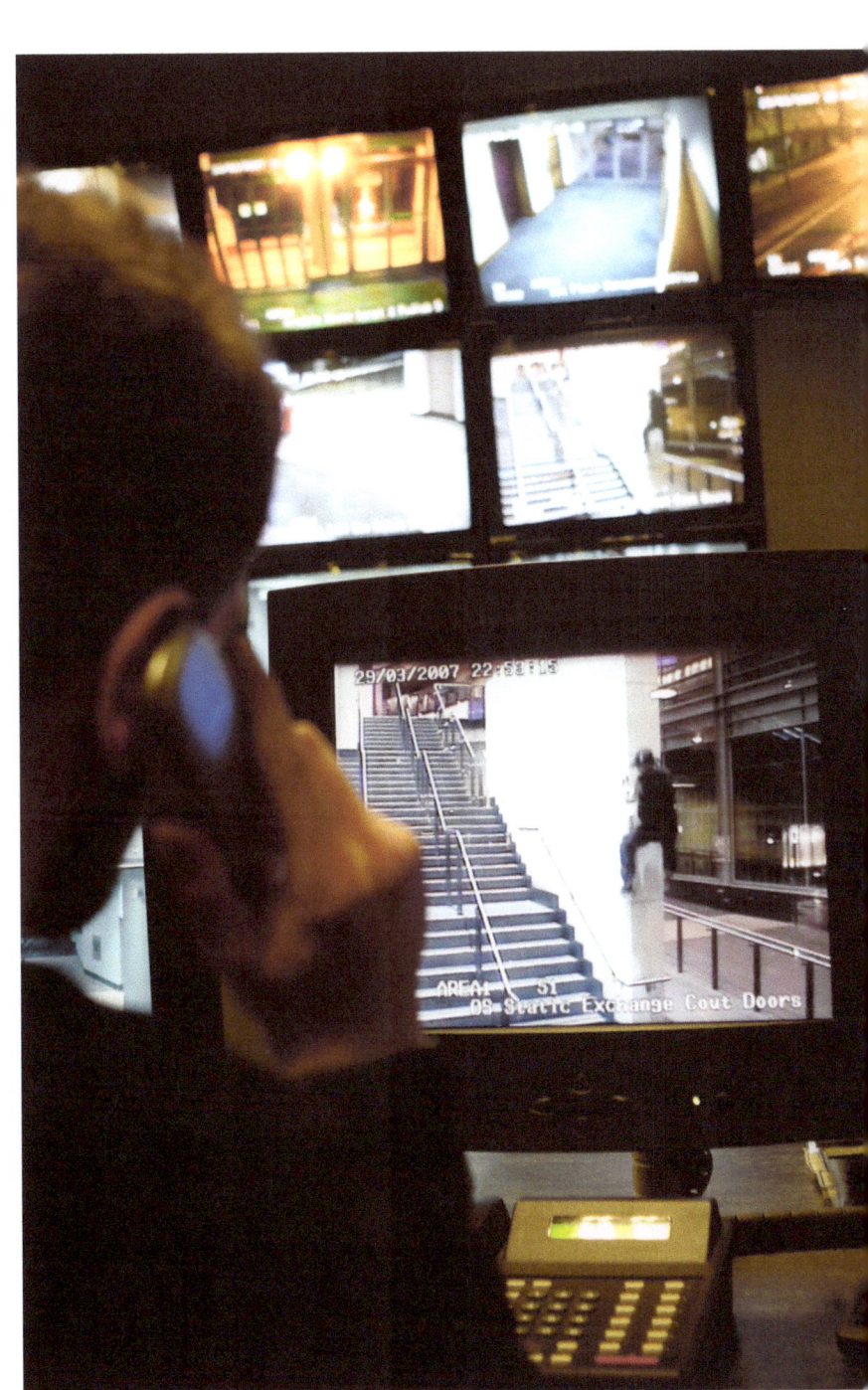

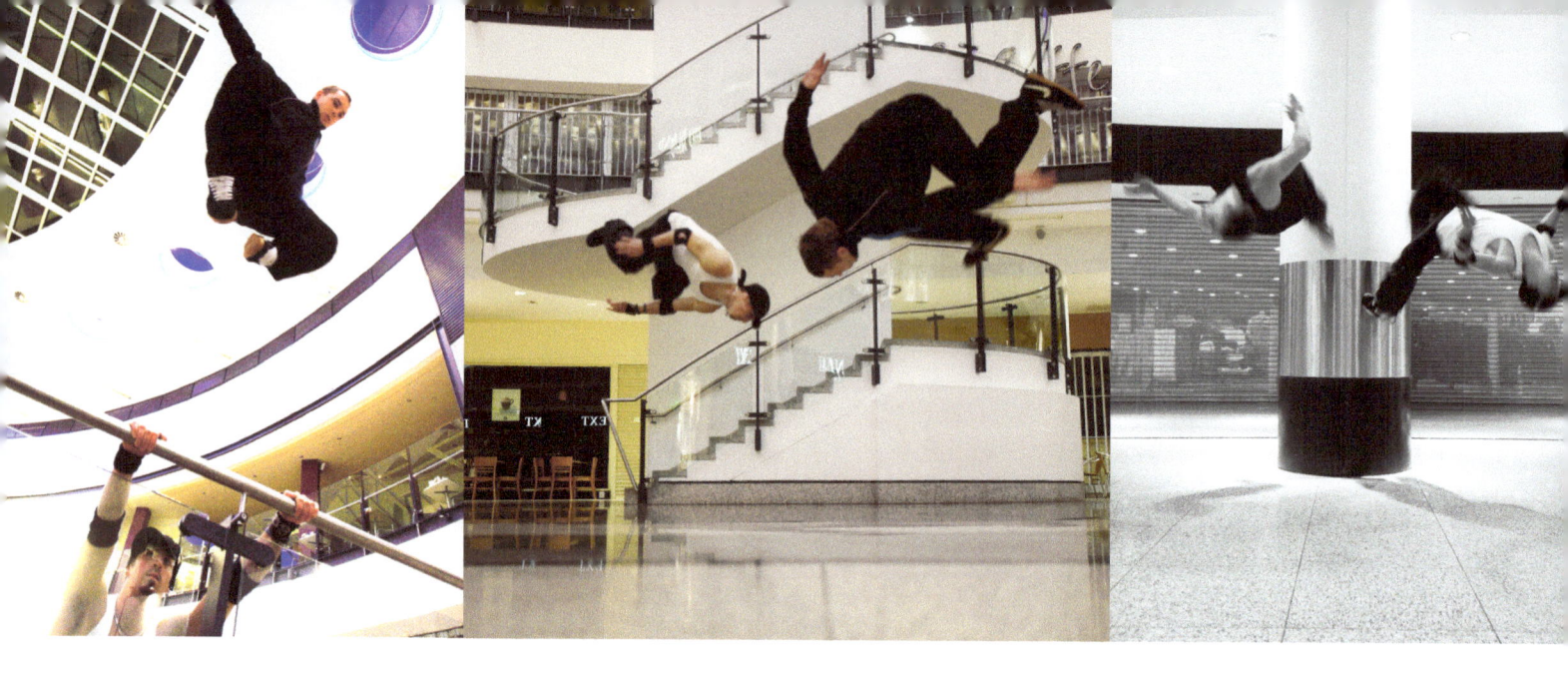

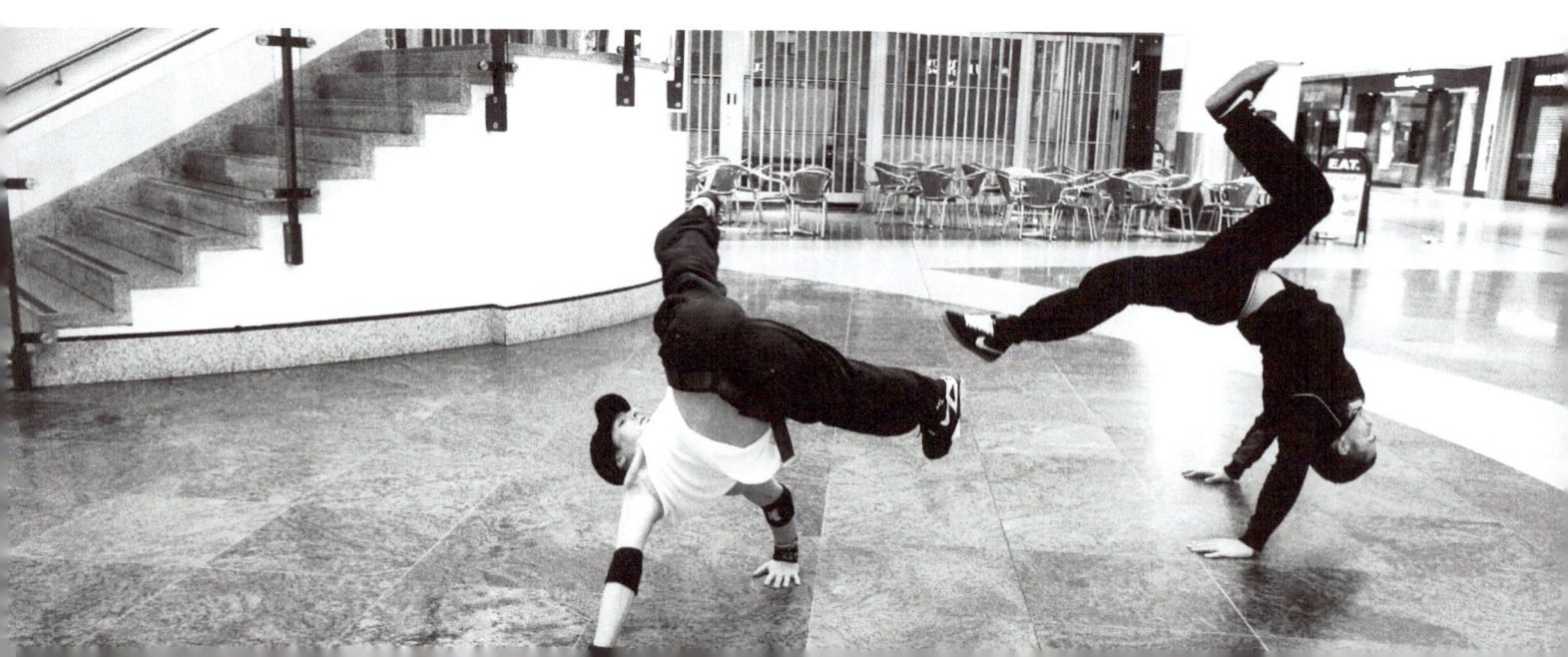

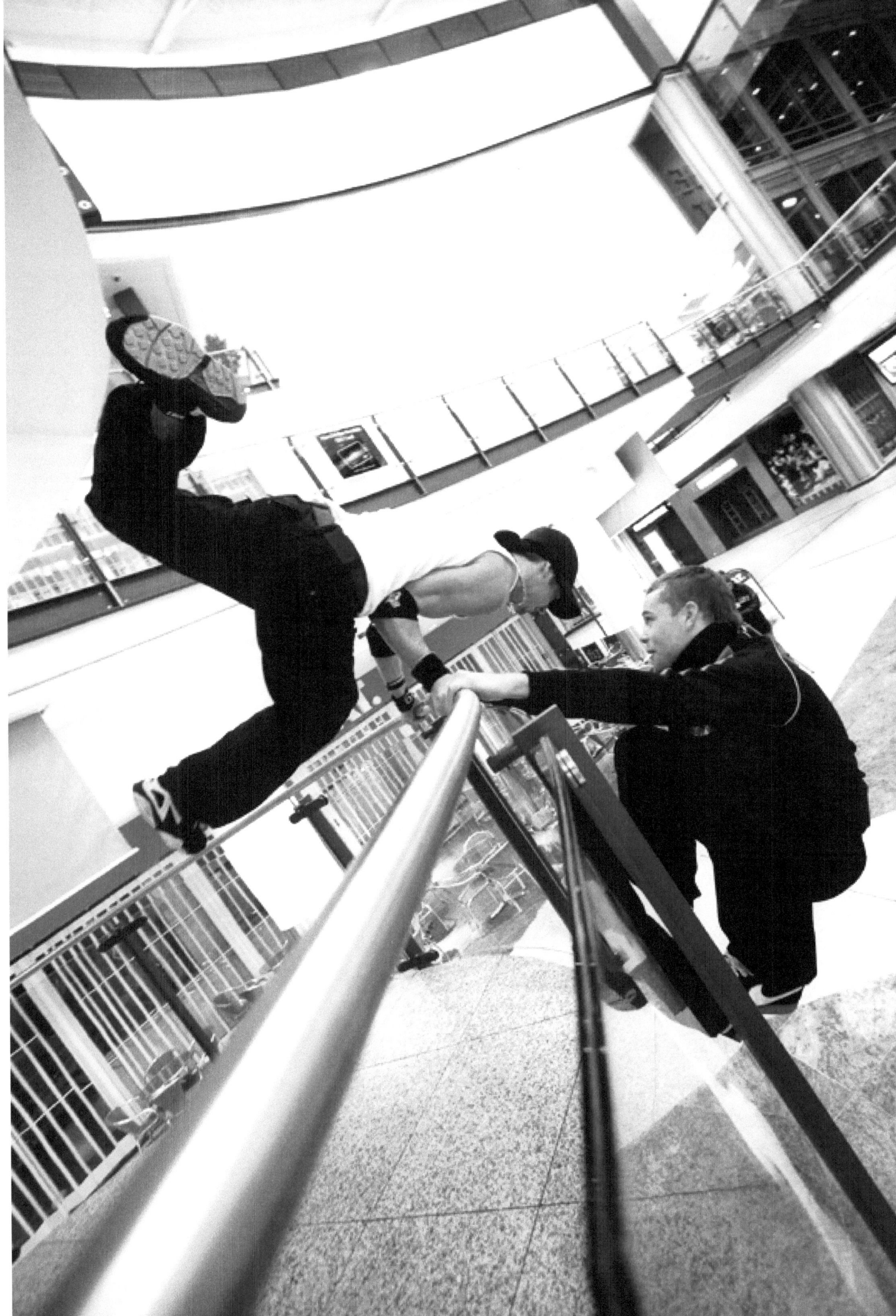

Trevor Paglen

Limit Telephotography

A number of military bases and installations exist in some of the remotest parts of the United States, hidden deep in western deserts and buffered by dozens of miles of restricted land. Many of these sites are so remote, in fact, that there is nowhere on Earth where a civilian might be able to see them with an unaided eye. In order to produce images of these remote and hidden landscapes, therefore, some unorthodox viewing and imaging techniques are required.

Limit-telephotography involves photographing landscapes that cannot be seen with the unaided eye. The technique employs high powered telescopes whose focal lengths range between 1300mm and 7000mm. At this level of magnification, hidden aspects of the landscape become apparent.

Limit-telephotography most closely resembles astrophotography, a technique that astronomers use to photograph objects that might be trillions of miles from Earth. In some ways, however, it is easier to photograph the depths of the solar system than it is to photograph the recesses of the military industrial complex. Between Earth and Jupiter (500 million miles away), for example, there are about five miles of thick, breathable atmosphere. In contrast, there are upwards of forty miles of thick atmosphere between an observer and the sites depicted in this series.

The Tonopah Test Range (TTR), near the town of Tonopah, NV was built in the 1940s to test rockets and missiles. In 1982, the facility underwent a huge amount of growth - over 70 hangars and support structures were added. The reason for these additions was that TTR became the designated home of the F-117 "stealth-fighter." The F-117 became operational in 1983, but remained secret until 1989 -- hence the need for a 'secret base' at Tonopah. Between 1983 and 1989, squadrons of stealth fighters traversed the Western and Midwestern United States, using unsuspecting people's houses as simulated targets in the dead of the night. The fighters were never flown during daylight hours until 1989, when the existence of the plane was declassified. Although the stealth-fighters moved to Holloman AFB in New Mexico in 1992, there is still a considerable amount of activity at TTR, but the nature of these activities is obscure. The Tonopah Test Range is jointly operated by Sandia National Laboratories, the Air Force, and the Department of Energy.

Missing Persons

Since the mid 1990s, the CIA has spearheaded a covert program to kidnap suspected terrorists from all over the world. These people are then brought to a network of secret CIA-operated prisons, called "black sites," where they are routinely tortured. The CIA calls this the "extraordinary rendition" program.

People taken to these secret prisons are effectively "disappeared": there are no public records of their captivity, their identities are kept secret, and they are prohibited from communicating with the outside world. Among CIA operatives, they are called "ghost detainees."

The locations of these black sites, known by code-names such as "Salt Pit" and "Bright Light," are some of the CIA's deepest secrets.

To capture and subsequently transport these ghost detainees, the CIA uses a fleet of unmarked airplanes. These airplanes are owned by intricate networks of front companies whose boards of directors are non-existent people. Missing Persons is a collection of their signatures culled from business records, aircraft registrations, and corporate filings.

< Trevor Paglen >

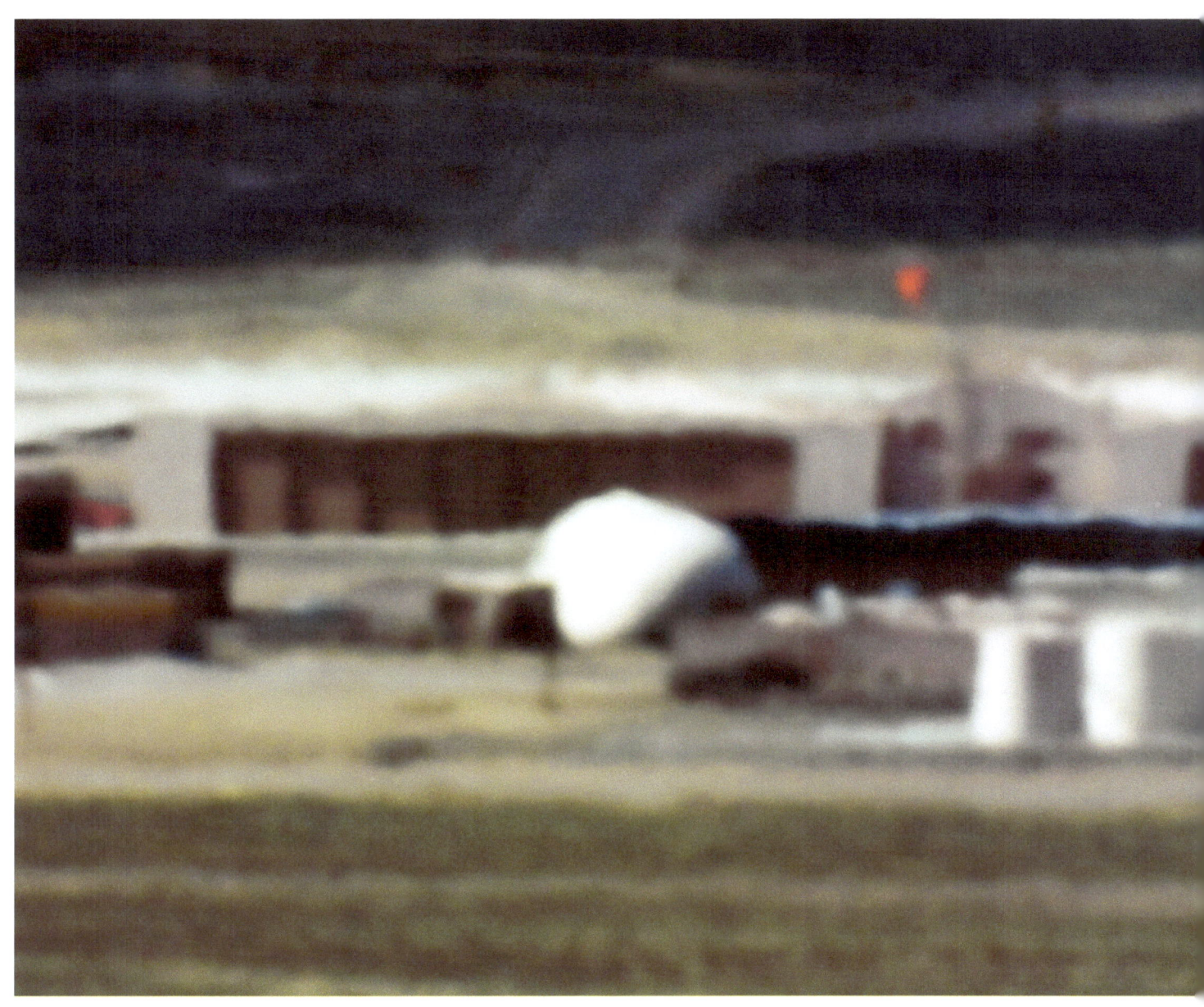

Large Hangars and Fuel Storage/Tonopah Test Range, NV/Distance ~18 miles/10:44 am, 2005
C-print 30 x 36 inches Edition 4/5

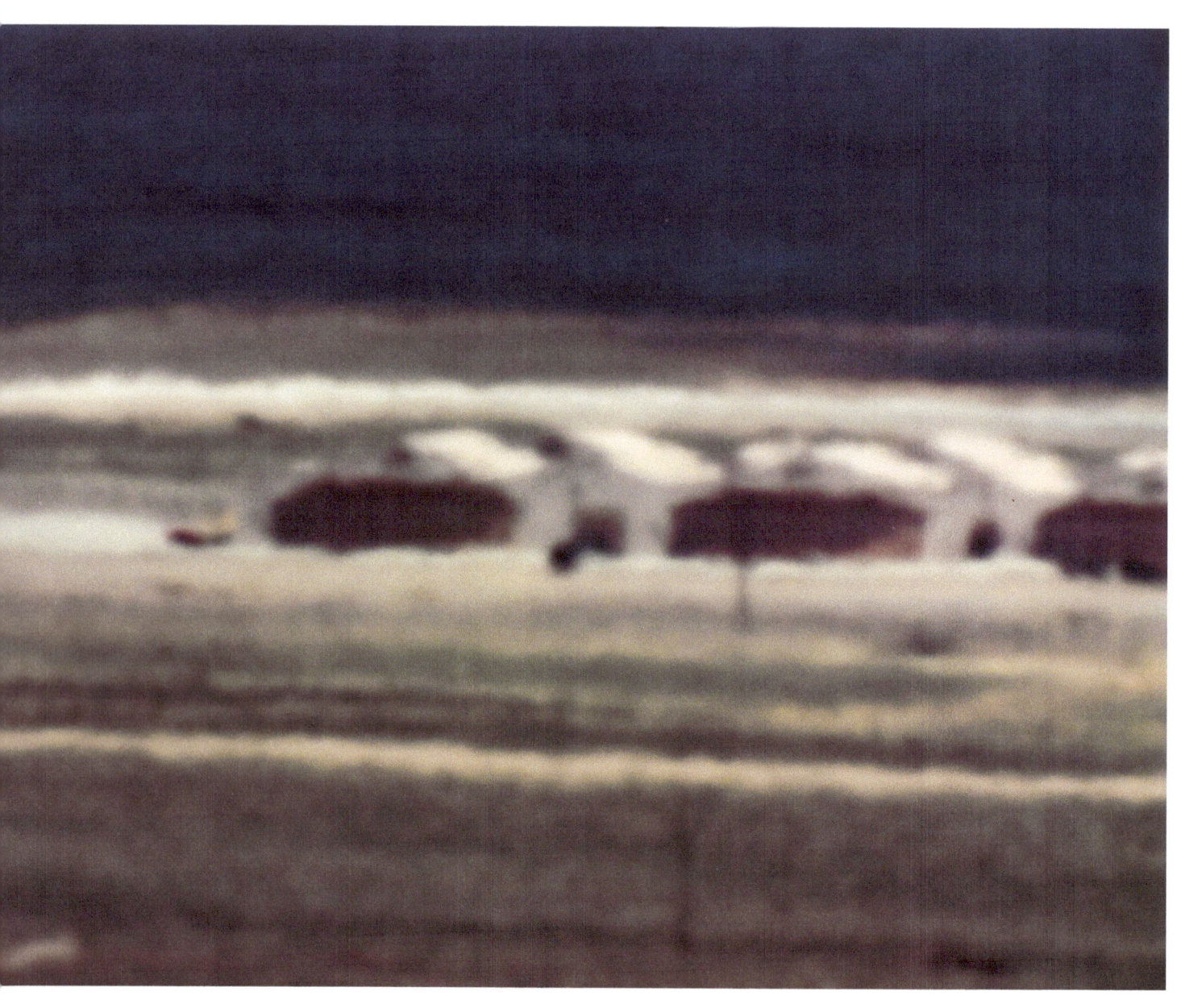

Canyons and Unidentified Vehicle/Tonopah Test Range, NV/Distance ~18 miles/12:45 pm, 2006
C-print 30 x 36 inches Edition 2/5

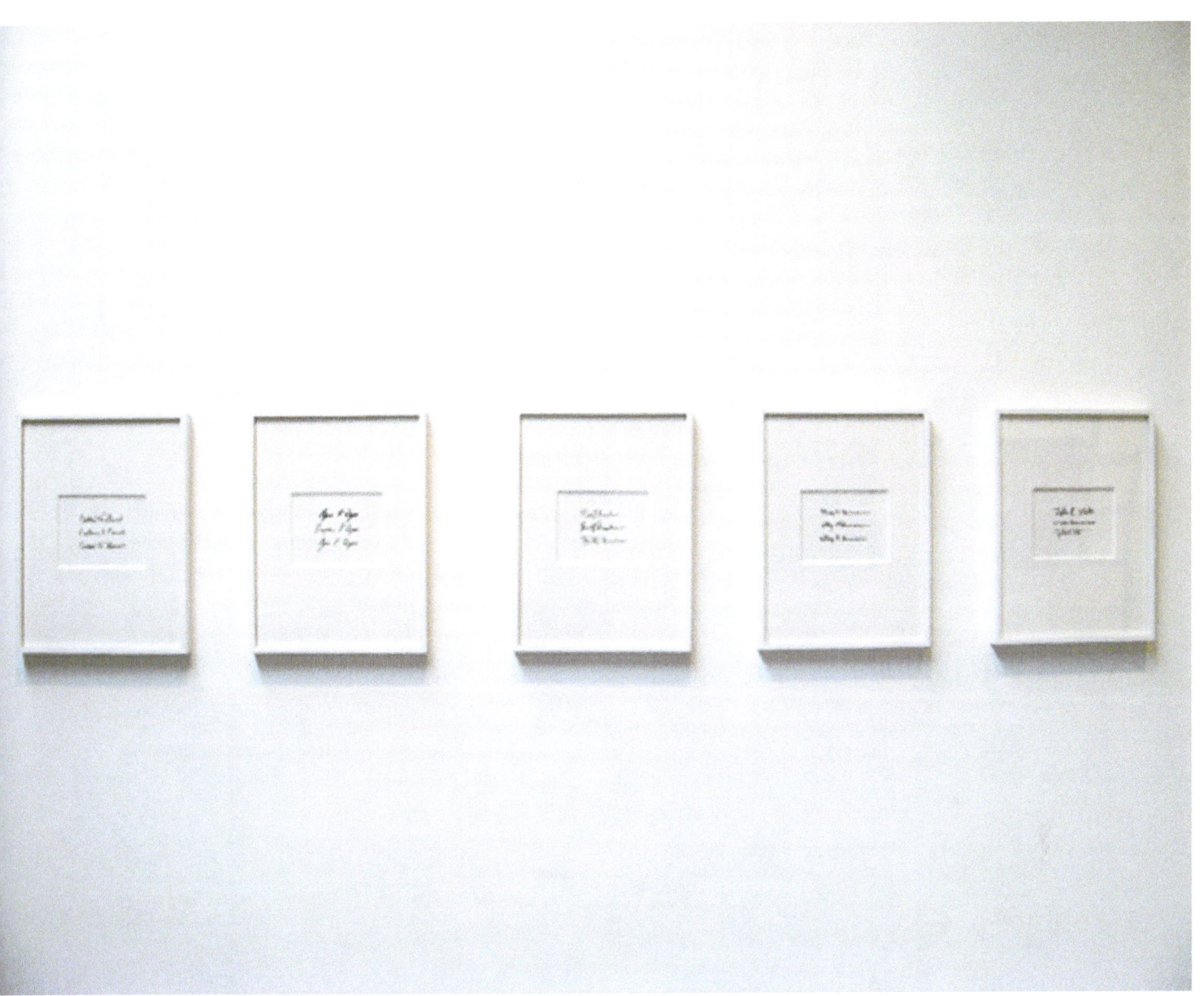

Missing Persons
Unique inkjet prints on archival paper, Set of 5, 2006

plan b

you, me and everywhere we go
plan b/ daniel belasco rogers and sophia new

beginnings: Dan began in 2003 obsessively mapping everywhere he's been with a GPS in an attempt to see the 'drawing of his life' and how he was getting to know a new city - Berlin. In 2007, the year our daughter, Ruby, began to walk, we said we'd map the distance between us when we are apart and the proximity when together. Soph began to record all of her movements too.

> The ordinary practitioners of the city live "down below," below the thresholds at which visibility begins. They walk - an elementary form of this experience of the city; they are walkers, *Wandersmänner*, whose bodies follow the thicks and thins of an urban "text" they write without being able to read it.[1]

birdseye view: looking down like a dizzy god on all those ignorant ants is not a perspective that everyone can have since what kept de Certeau aloft (seeing Manhattan from the 110th floor of the World Trade Centre) was destroyed in front of our (square) eyes on that September 11th. Perhaps it's an attempt to shake a fist at that omnipotent eye that we began to try and make sense of our own illiterate wanderings across an (increasingly Google) earth that can now be rolled under our cursors like a blue marble. To be the readers of our own urban text.

down on the ground: what happens when you do this for a while you realise that this is not like a text at all. Your 'handwriting' is constrained by the cities' streets, you can't write what you want. We've come to think of this now as a rubbing. In the same way as rubbing a tombstone is a record of time and proximity to the stone, our marks recorded across a city and across thousands of hours of time ultimately reveal the shape of those streets and reveal a recognisable city layout. A rough rubbing that is affected by the shadows of buildings and GPS inaccuracies (at best 5 meters) - we are in the lap of the satellites now.

shifting position: many people want to know if we go somewhere on purpose because we're recording everything. If we see a blank space on the drawings and think 'I must go there'. This reveals an underlying question that is a lot more difficult to deny - does the knowledge of recording your movements affect your journeys? The initial intention is to record our everyday movements and so not make special journeys just to draw lines. However, having to remember a GPS every time you leave the house, having to have a pocket full of

batteries on longer excursions and remember to download tracks every two weeks of so. No, we can't forget about

this practice. But then why would we want to? It's taken a long time to develop a feeling for the shape of our lives but I'm not about to draw a shape on an open space.

reflections: I think the hardest part for me was the trip I made to Japan. Not only was I seeing something extraordinary without you and missing you both like an amputated limb, the jet lag had made me extremely emotional. Remember the tearful phone call when I finally got through in the middle of my unfamiliar night and your workaday morning? < Dan >

that's why those text messages became so relevant: the link and communication of the distance between us. journeys together are marked by an absence of text.

I was very aware of the lines I was making on the first walks with, Ruby, as she led me every so slowly on a twisty turny journey by the canal in Kreuzberg. She was not going from A to B but exploring the world from moment to moment, side tracked by small stones, acorns, bottle tops and dogs. My GPS made a lot of points that day and distance was condensed into a dance of back and forth rather than from here to there. < Soph >

[1] Michel de Certeau, *The Practice of Everyday Life.* (Steven Rendall. Trans.) University of California Press, 1984, p.93

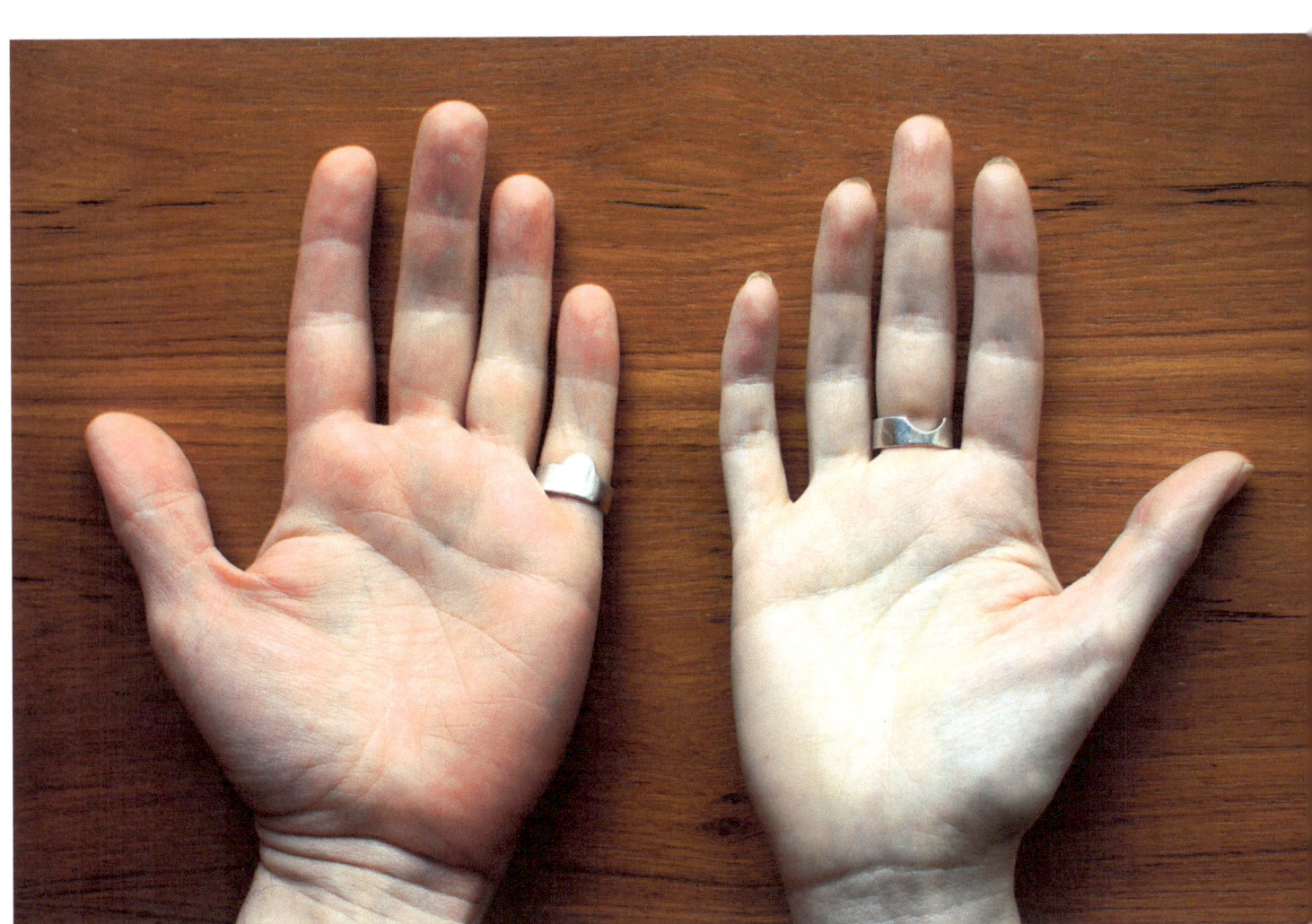

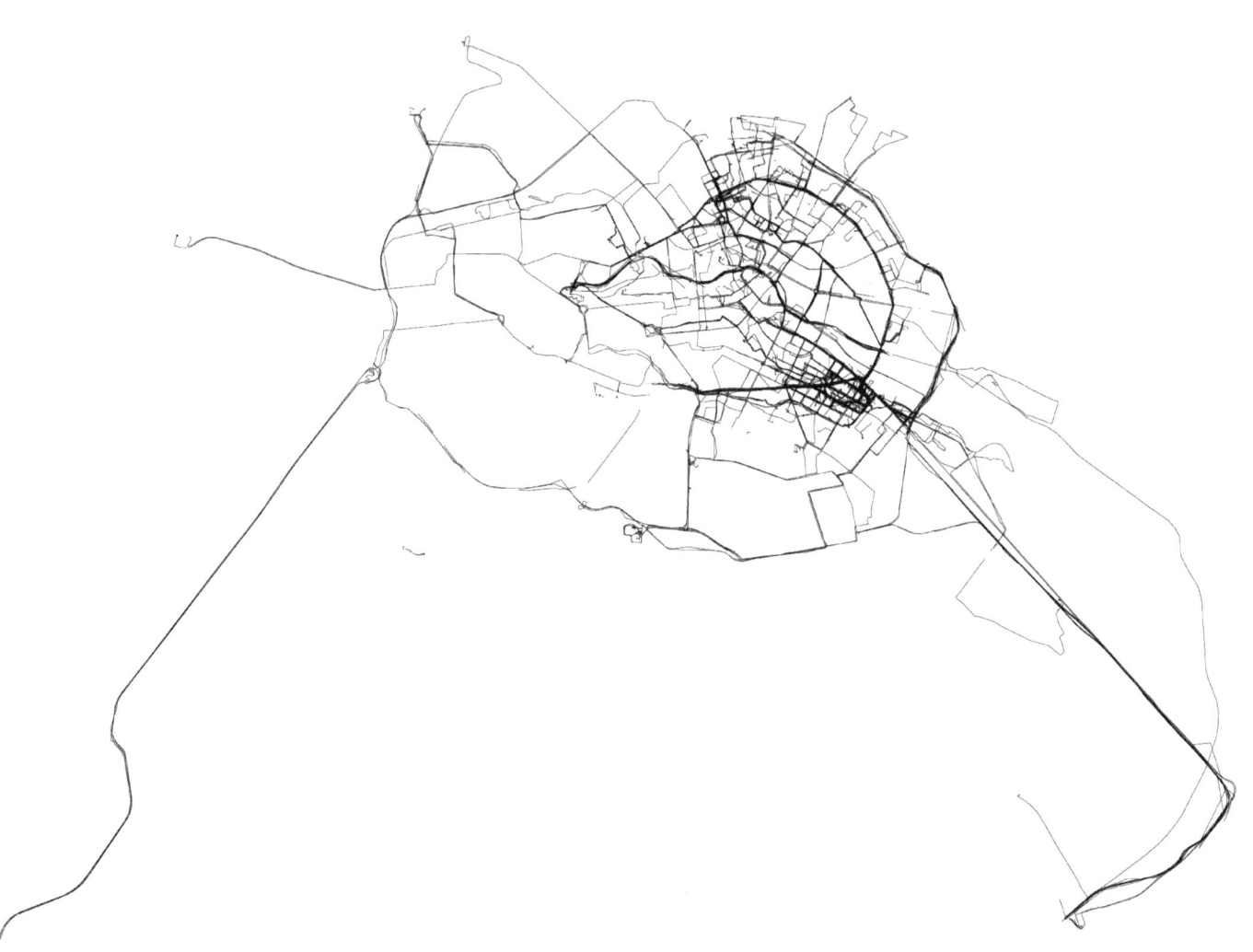

One Year Drawing 2007 Berlin   Daniel Belasco Rogers

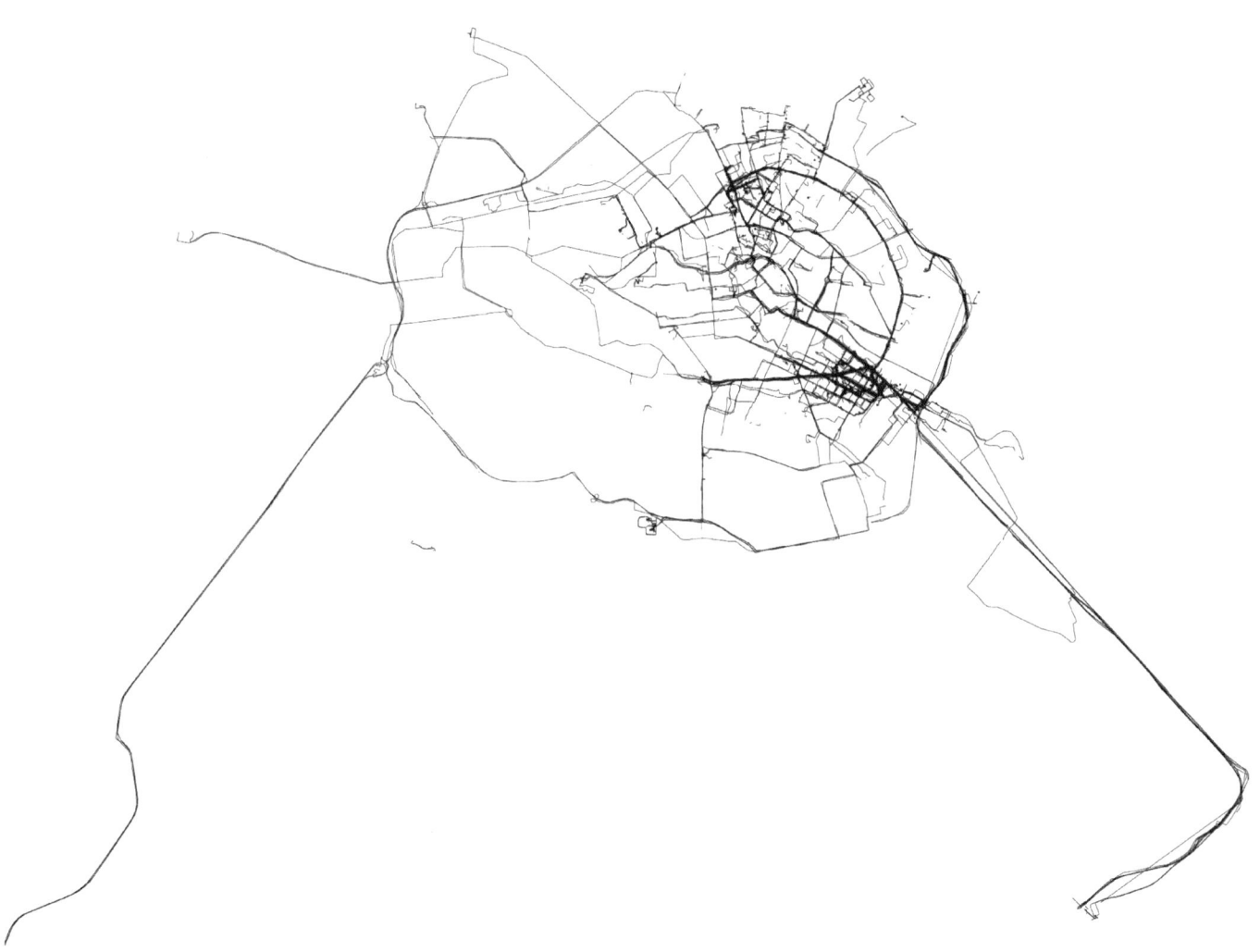

One Year Drawing 2007 Berlin   Sophia New

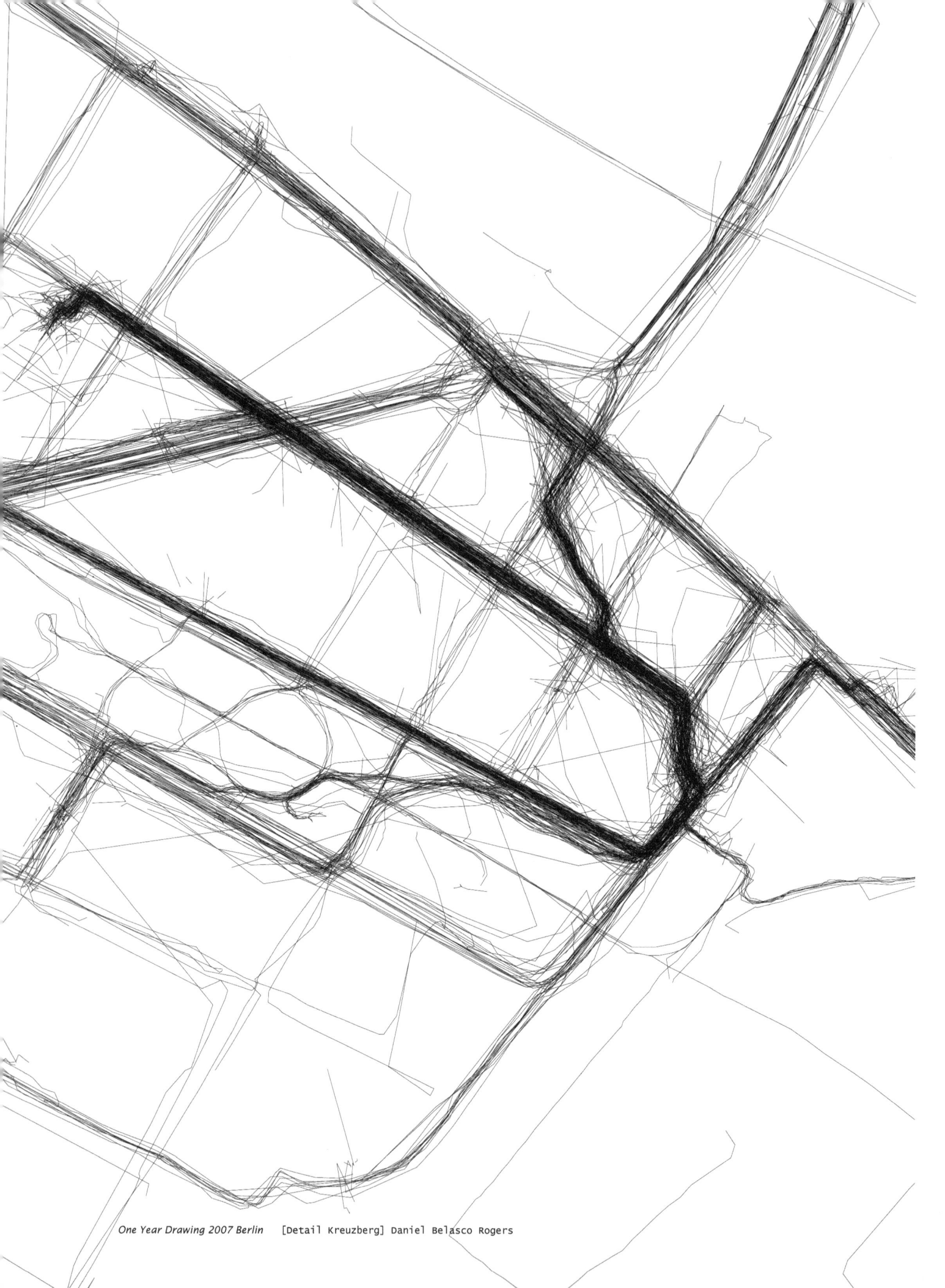

One Year Drawing 2007 Berlin [Detail Kreuzberg] Daniel Belasco Rogers

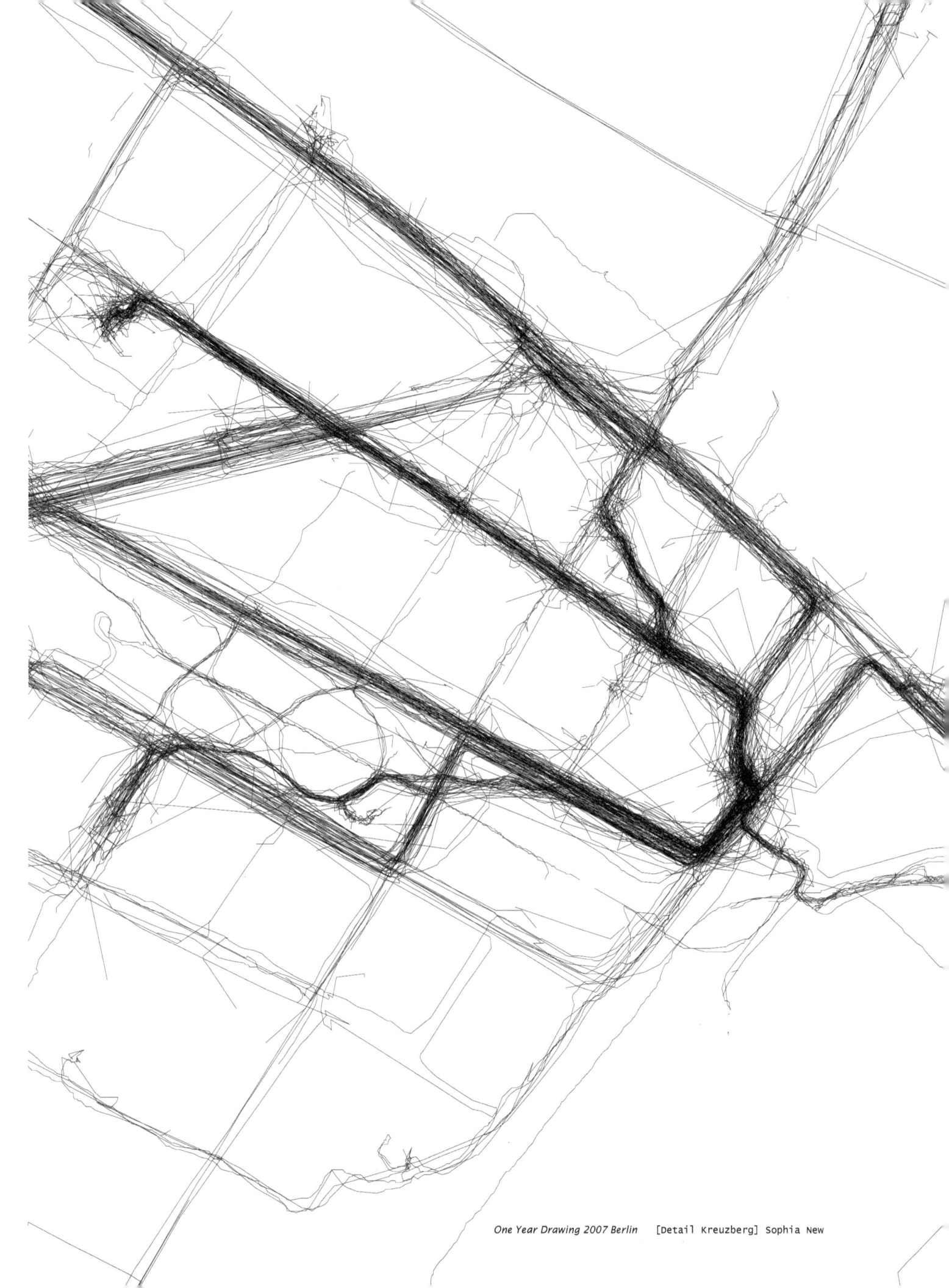

One Year Drawing 2007 Berlin [Detail Kreuzberg] Sophia New

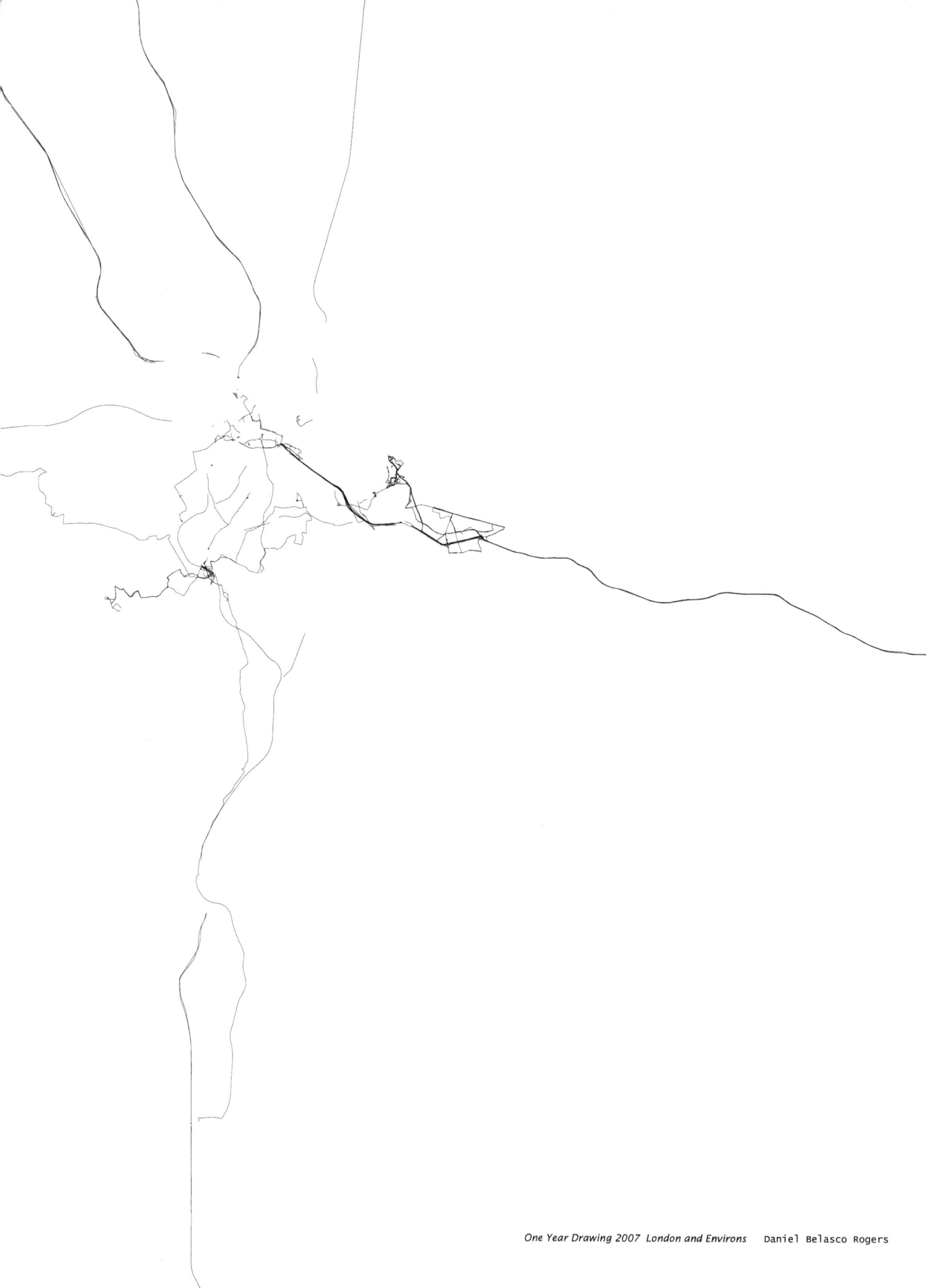

One Year Drawing 2007 London and Environs Daniel Belasco Rogers

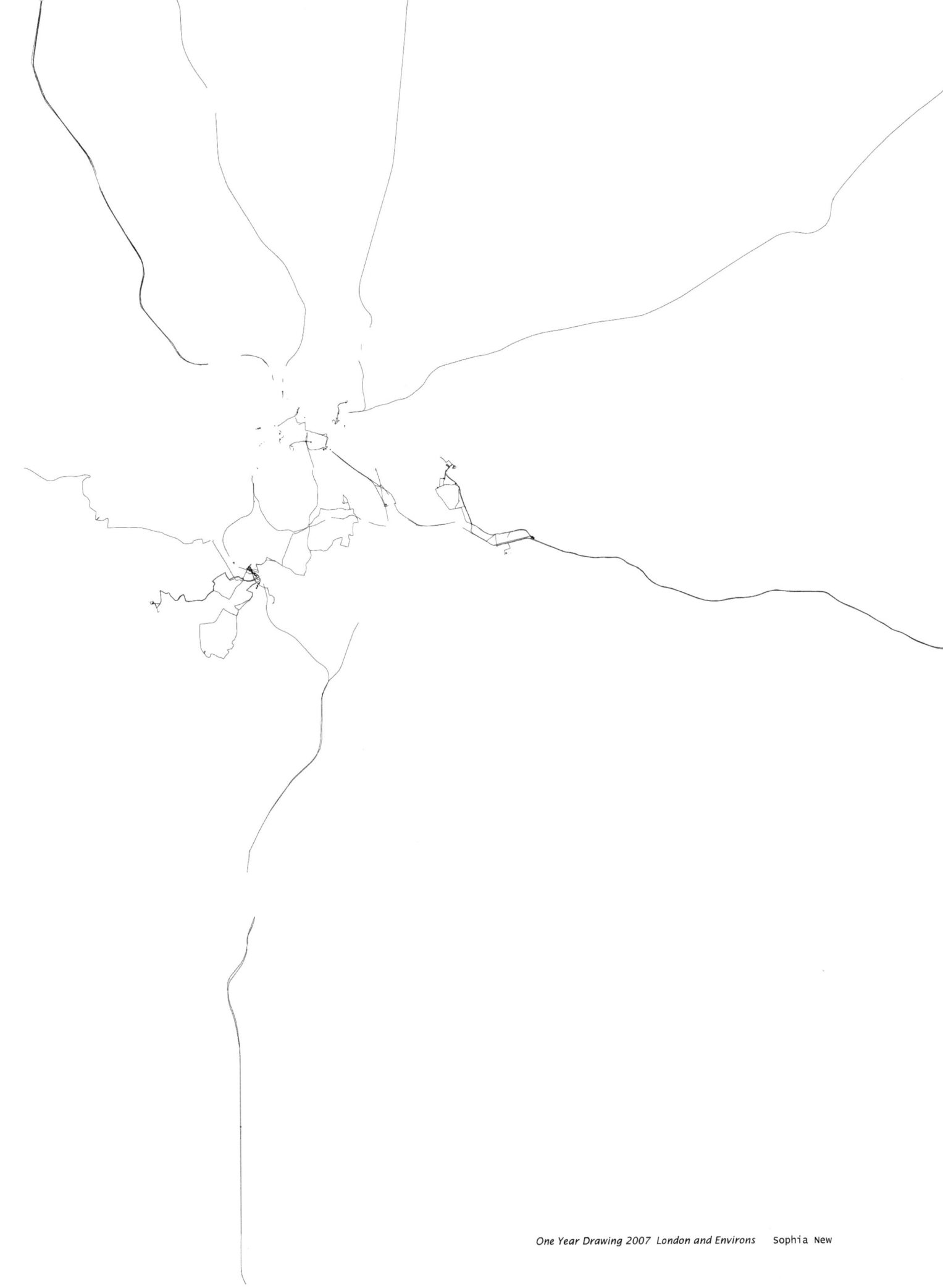

One Year Drawing 2007 London and Environs   Sophia New

How's it going today? I'm having a break with Timo and eating xxx
Sent:
13:57:33
27-11-2007

Nicole still feels ill. Ruby cried when i left. Dentist painful but worth it have to go back same day as you. Need another op on legs, have app in jan. S x
Sent:
14:06:36
27:11:2007

Good to hear. I'm at the academy, looking round. Have delivered work back home. Love you xxx
Sent:
12:35:49
08-01-2008

Have arrived. All good. Having coffee. Going to get bus as it going to victoria which is easier. Hope your day going well. Love soph sorry i have ruby's gloves!
Sent:
12:33:02
08-01-2008

We're all clear, she can go to kita tomorrow xxx
Sent:
11:43:38
28-11-2007

Go mad! I love you xxx
Sent:
11:49:14
28-11-2007

Will you text me when i can call you? I miss not talking. Everything good here xxx
Sent:
19:53:00
09-01-2008

We could do with some bread and if there's anything in the bakers that would do for lunch. She isn't hungry but i'll try and put her down soon xxx
Sent:
13:09:54
28-11-2007

On way home now perhaps you could call me there in 30 mins. Lots of love s x kiss rubes for me.
Sent:
20:49:44
09-01-2008

Can you tell of again what I need to put into mail 2 web. Forgot again! S x
Sent:
11:25:07
10-01-2008

How was she. I just got out from docs. She was nice it was unpleasant. All problems = my fear. Hard pill to swallow. Soph x
Sent:
11:32:19
30-11-2007

Go to planbperformance. net/webmail and put in your email address and your password xxx
Sent:
11:28:33
10-01-2008

Did you get monika.s message? I think that's round the corner. Text her back? xxx
Sent:
15:31:14
30-11-2007

Starting journey back to you! Mum just came to victoria with me & was very teary. Hope you ok today. Love soph x
Sent:
16:37:09
10-01-2008

Yup round corner. Suggest tomorrow? At ours when ruby asleep? Love s x have to ruby can you do it?
Sent:
15:48:24
30-11-2007

Can't wait to see you. Ruby happy xxx
Sent:
17:01:32
10-01-2008

On way back now xxx
Sent:
17:05:56
30-11-2007

Big stress to get to airport. what was name of novel with gps? S x
Sent:
18:59:51
10-01-2008

It's called spook country. Are you ok? xxx
Sent:
19:02:46
10-01-2008

Just had idea. Maybe I could go dancing at lido with han later at 23.oo. If i can stay awake. I hope it is good tonight. S x
Sent:
18:55:35
01-12-2007

Darling just arrived. Could you check out quickest way for me to get home to you. Had no time to get book in the end sorry. Love s x
Sent:
21:21:17
10-01-2008

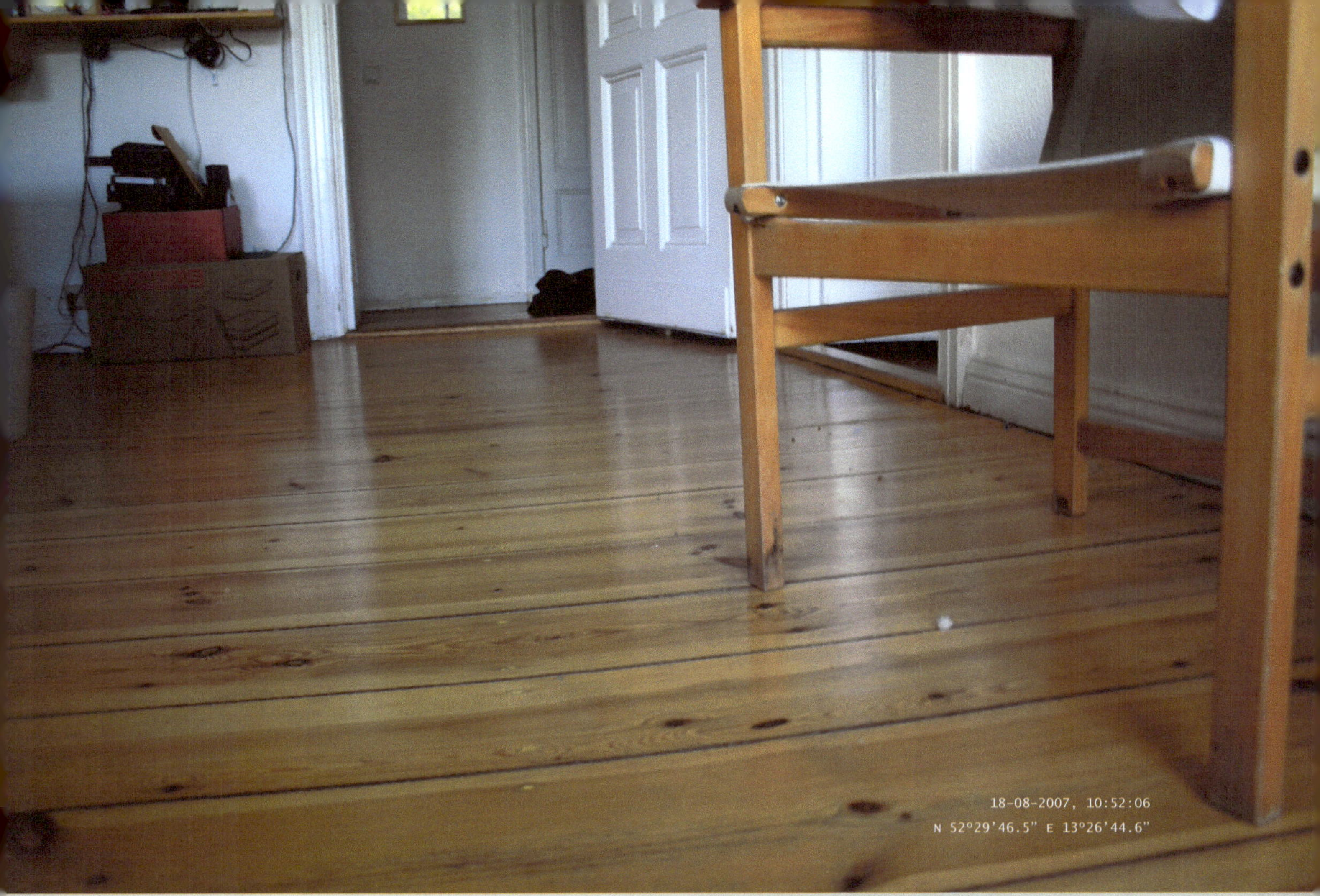

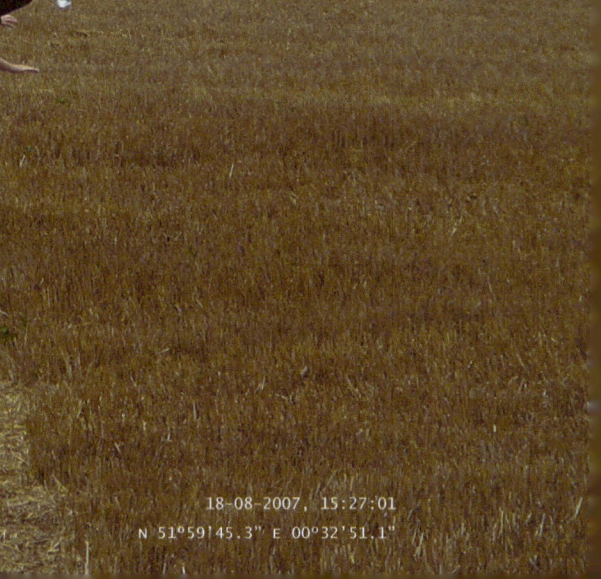

18-08-2007, 10:52:06
N 52°29'46.5" E 13°26'44.6"

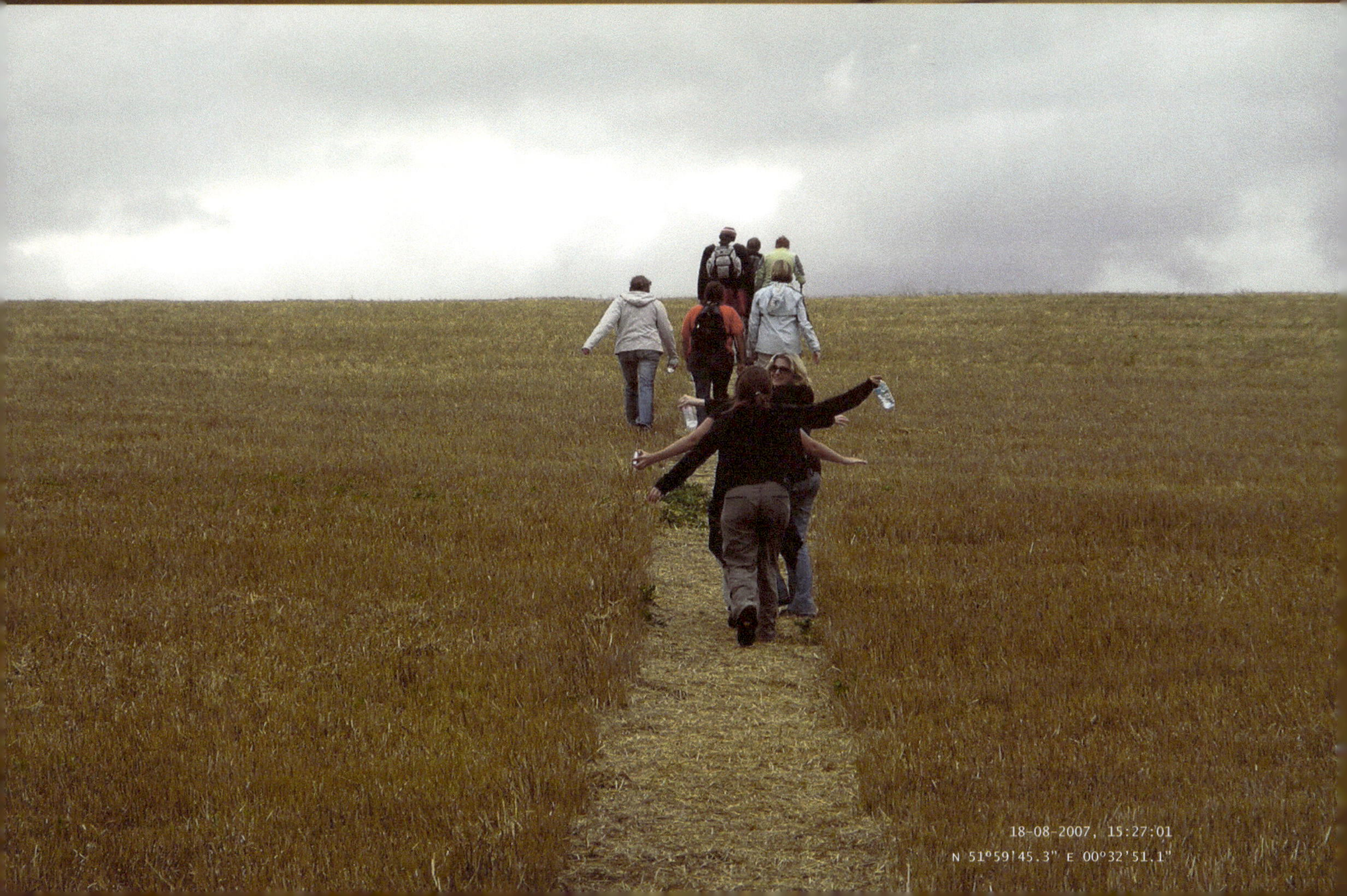

18-08-2007, 15:27:01
N 51°59'45.3" E 00°32'51.1"

RYbN

antidatamining

CAC 40|4618.96|-1.26|-17.73
BEL 20|3635.06|-1.04|-11.93
NASDAQ COMPOSITE|2212.49|-0.36|-16.58
Hang Seng|22501.3|-3.6|-19.1
SMI|7174.15|-1.32|-15.44
S&P/TSX|13281.7|-0.59|-3.99
MIB 30|32823|-1.73|-15.59
Ibex35|12677.8|-0.98|-16.5
TECHN. ALL SHARE|913.17|-2.39|-23.87
NASDAQ 100|1707.5|-0.29|-18.1
DOW JONES INDU.|11893.7|-1.22|-10.34
AEX 25|434.81|-0.56|-15.7
DAX Xetra|6499.2|-1.4|-19.44
FTSE 100|5699.9|-1.15|-11.72
SP 500|1293.35|-0.84|-11.92
Nikkei 225|12782.8|-3.27|-16.49

AEGON|9.15|-1.08
AHOLD KON|9.1|-0.11
AKZO NOBEL|52.62|0.82
ARCELORMITTAL|49.5|-2.37
ASML HOLDING|15.63|0.39
CORPORATE EXPRESS|7.61|-2.31
DSM KON|28.04|-2.87
FORTIS|14.77|3.29
HAGEMEYER|4.83|0.21
HEINEKEN|36.71|-1.1
ING GROEP|20.93|-1.23
KPN KON|12.4|0.73
PHILIPS KON|25.42|-1.01
RANDSTAD|24.88|0.28
REED ELSEVIER|12.24|2.94
ROYAL DUTCH SHELLA|22.41|-1.41
SBM OFFSHORE|19.43|-2.17
TNT|24.46|-1.25
TOMTOM|28.08|-4.85
UNIBAIL-RODAMCO|166.74|-2.27
UNILEVER|20.32|0.54
VEDIOR|16.83|-0.65
WOLTERS KLUWER|17.34|1.11

PHILIPS KON

2 AMSTELPLEIN PO BOX
77900 1070 MX AMSTERDAM PAYS-BAS

PLACE BOURSIÈRE :
AEX

VARIATION EN % :
-1.01

SECTEUR D'ACTIVITÉ :
ELECTRICITE ELECTRONIQUE

COUR ACTUEL :
25.42

CAPITALISATION BOURSIÈRE :
2.90505e+10

CHIFFRE D'AFFAIRE :
2.6793e+10

RÉSULTAT NET :
4.173e+09

NOMBRE DE TITRES :
1.14282e+09

DIRIGEANTS :
PRESIDENT AND CHIEF EXECUTIVE OFFICER : M
VICE PRESIDENT : MONSIEUR GOTTFRIED DUTII
EXECUTIVE VICE-PRESIDENT : MONSIEUR RUDY
EXECUTIVE VICE-PRESIDENT : MADAME ANDRE.
EXECUTIVE VICE-PRESIDENT : MONSIEUR STEVI
EXECUTIVE VICE-PRESIDENT : MONSIEUR THEC
FINANCES : MONSIEUR PIERRE-JEAN SIVIGNON

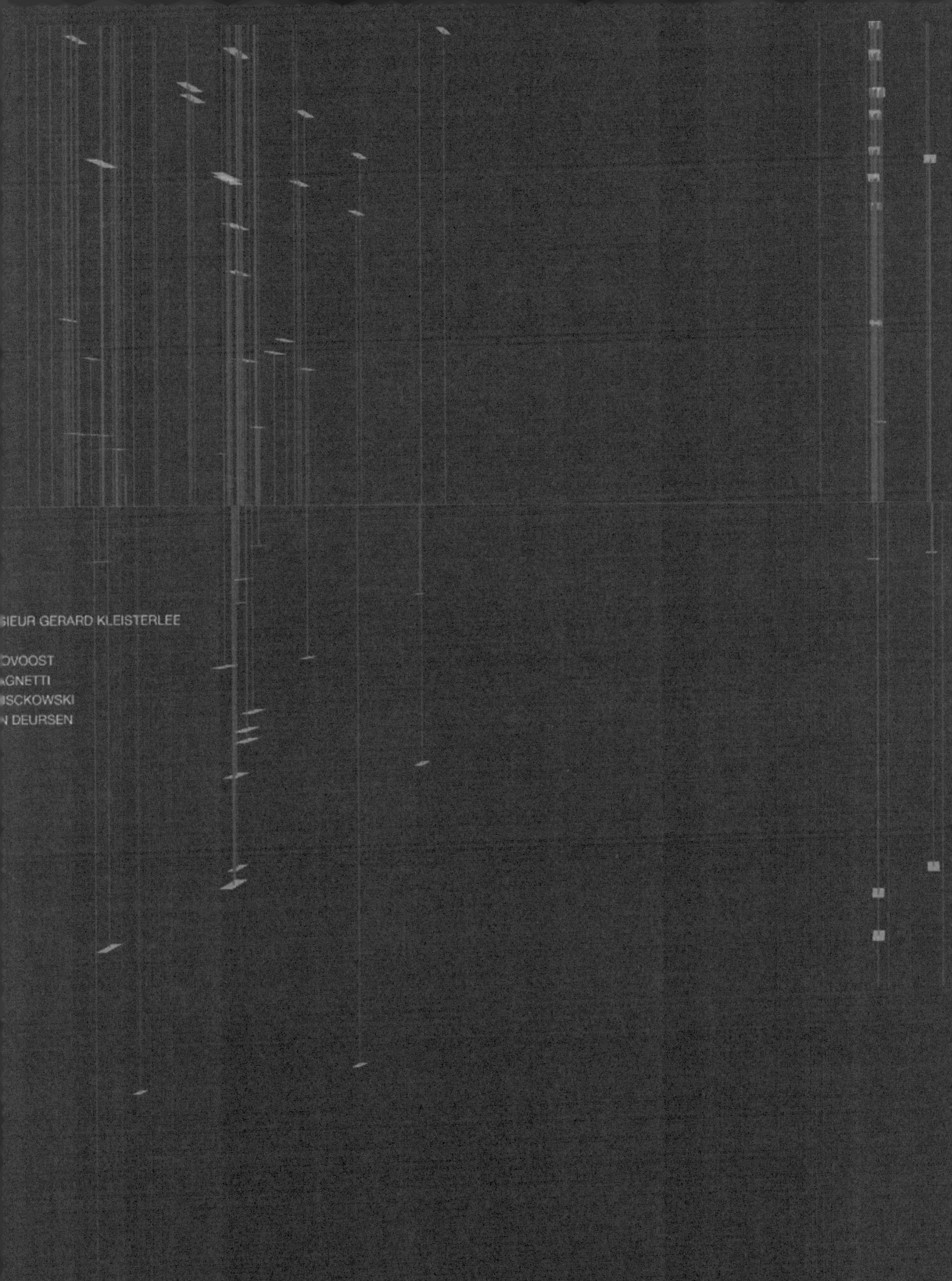

GIEUR GERARD KLEISTERLEE

OVOOST
AGNETTI
ISCKOWSKI
N DEURSEN

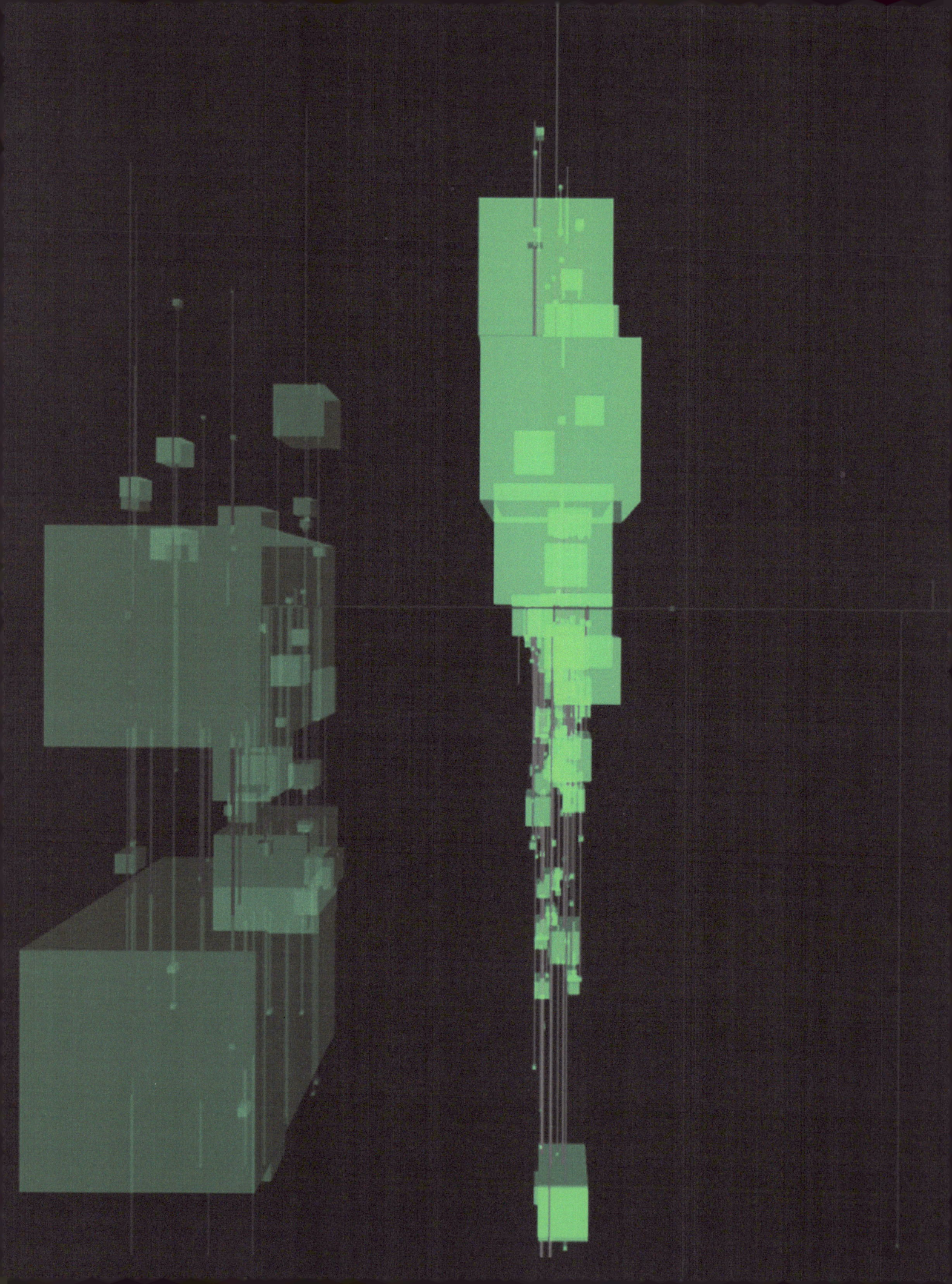

skúta

Happy Feet in Aberdeen

A two-part surveillance project
Part One
Peacock Visual Arts /
Earl Of Sandwich

Part Two
University of Aberdeen cafeteria the Hub /
Recoded website and conference

Bringing the surveillance camera down from its
superior height

By repositioning a surveillance camera to a "child's
eye" view (vulnerable position), from the standard
"bird's eye" view (parental/authority position),
prompting surveillance subjects to question the
social invisibility of surveillance.

Part One: a live surveillance exchange between
Peacock Visual Arts and Earl of Sandwich
take-away. At the entrance to Peacock Visual Arts a
camera positioned just above the floor recorded the
passing of people, providing surveillance of the
lower legs as they entered and exited. The camera
recording was presented in real time on a video
screen located on the wall behind the counter at
Earl of Sandwich, facing customers as they entered.
In the same manner surveillance was streamed from
Earl of Sandwich to Peacock Visual Arts.

Part Two: a direct link to the Recoded website and
conference. A surveillance camera recorded traffic
at the University of Aberdeen campus cafeteria, The
Hub. The camera was positioned inside the entrance
to the cafeteria, streaming passing foot traffic
to the Recoded website. During the conference,
streaming from the cafeteria was projected in
the intervals when speakers were not using the
conference screen.

< skúta >

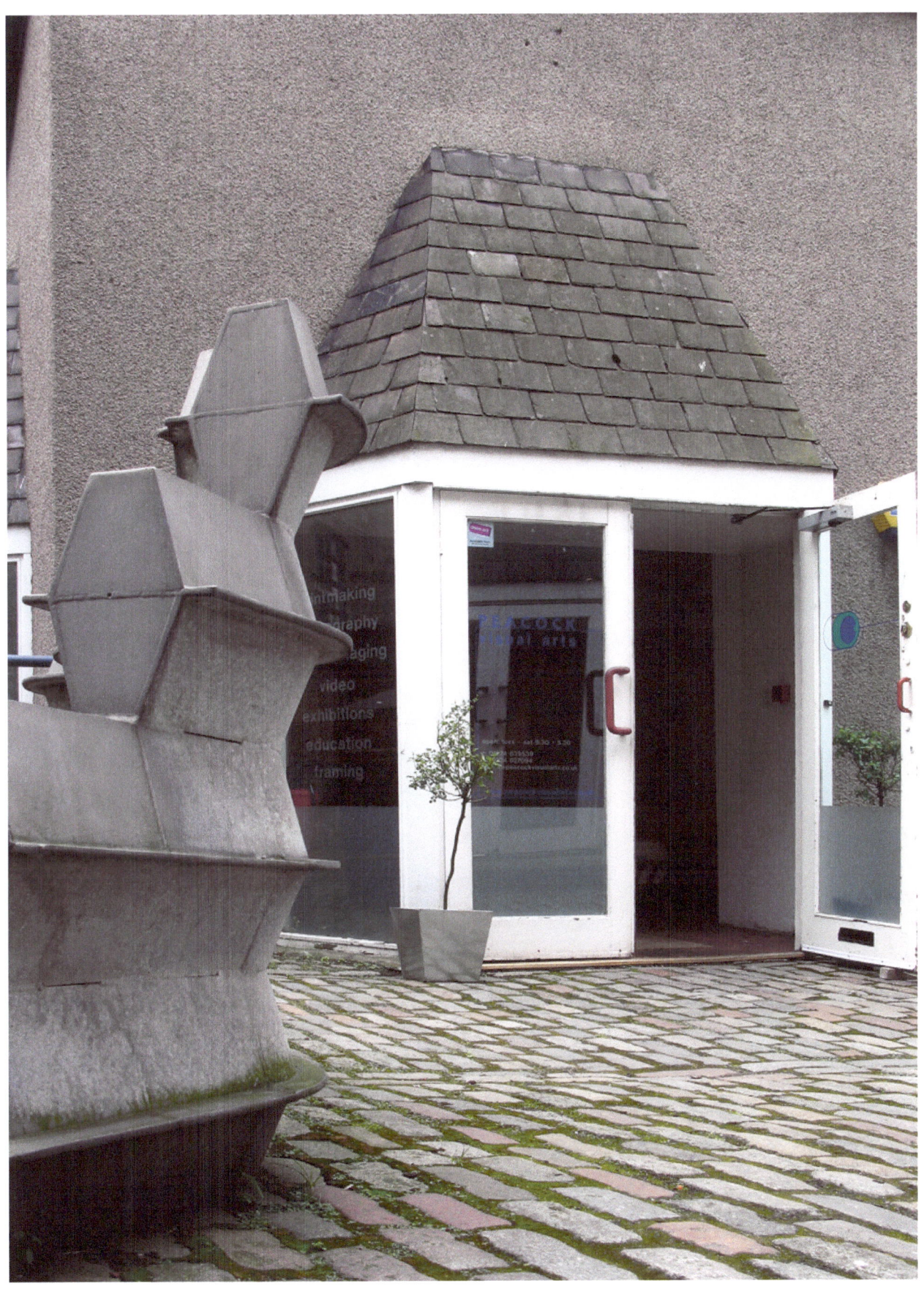

Happy Feet in Aberdeen
Part One
Peacock Visual Arts /
Earl Of Sandwich

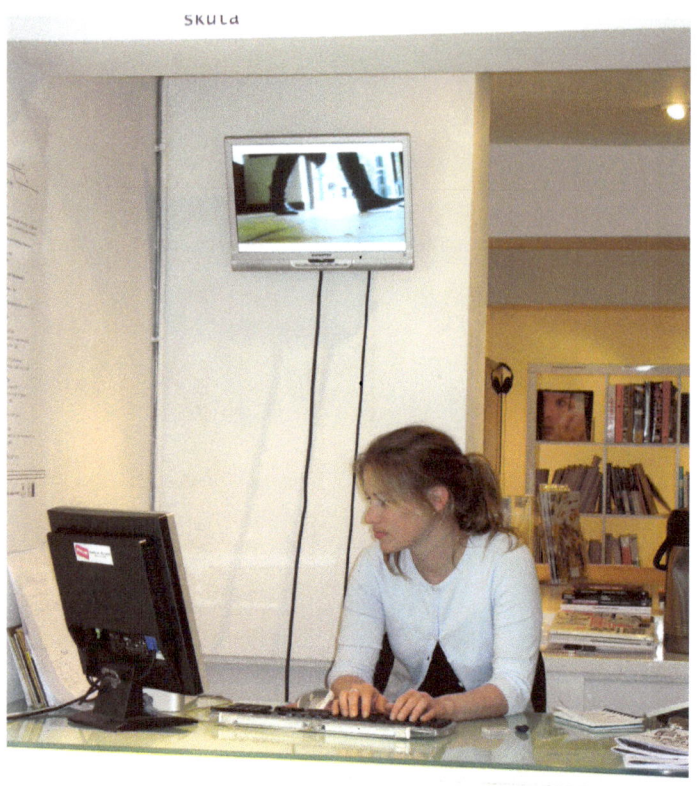

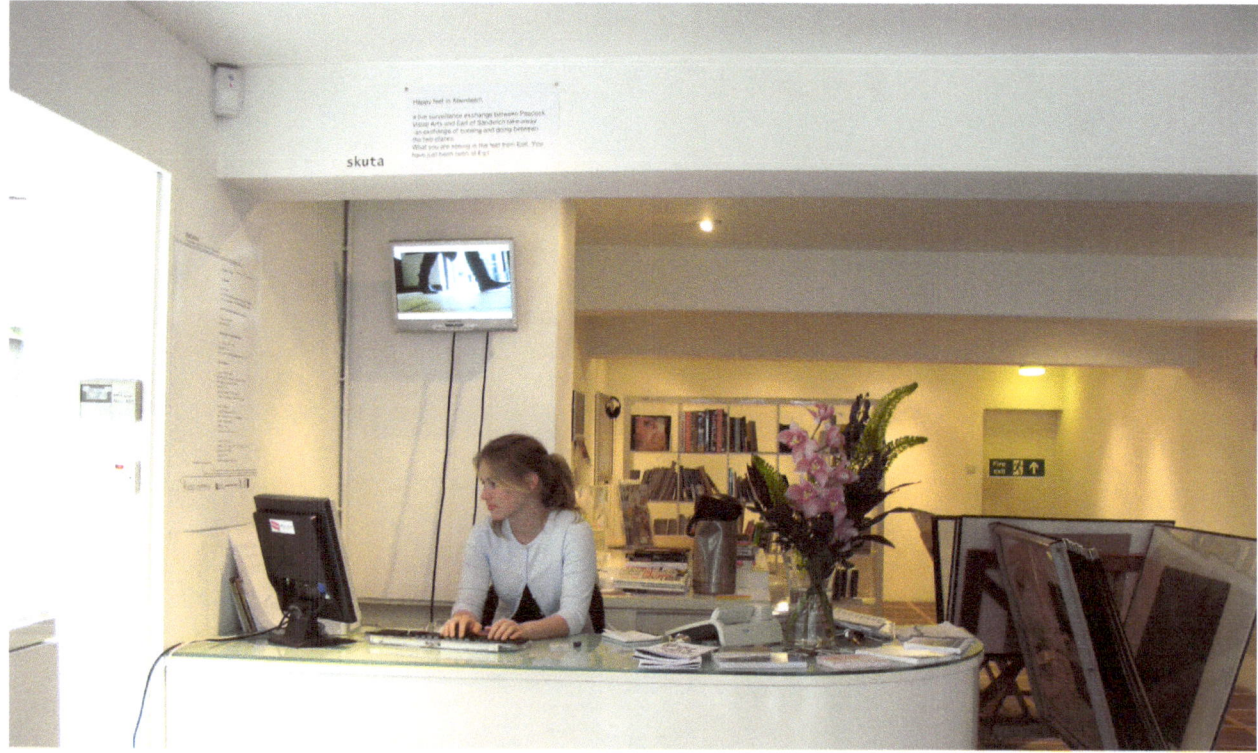

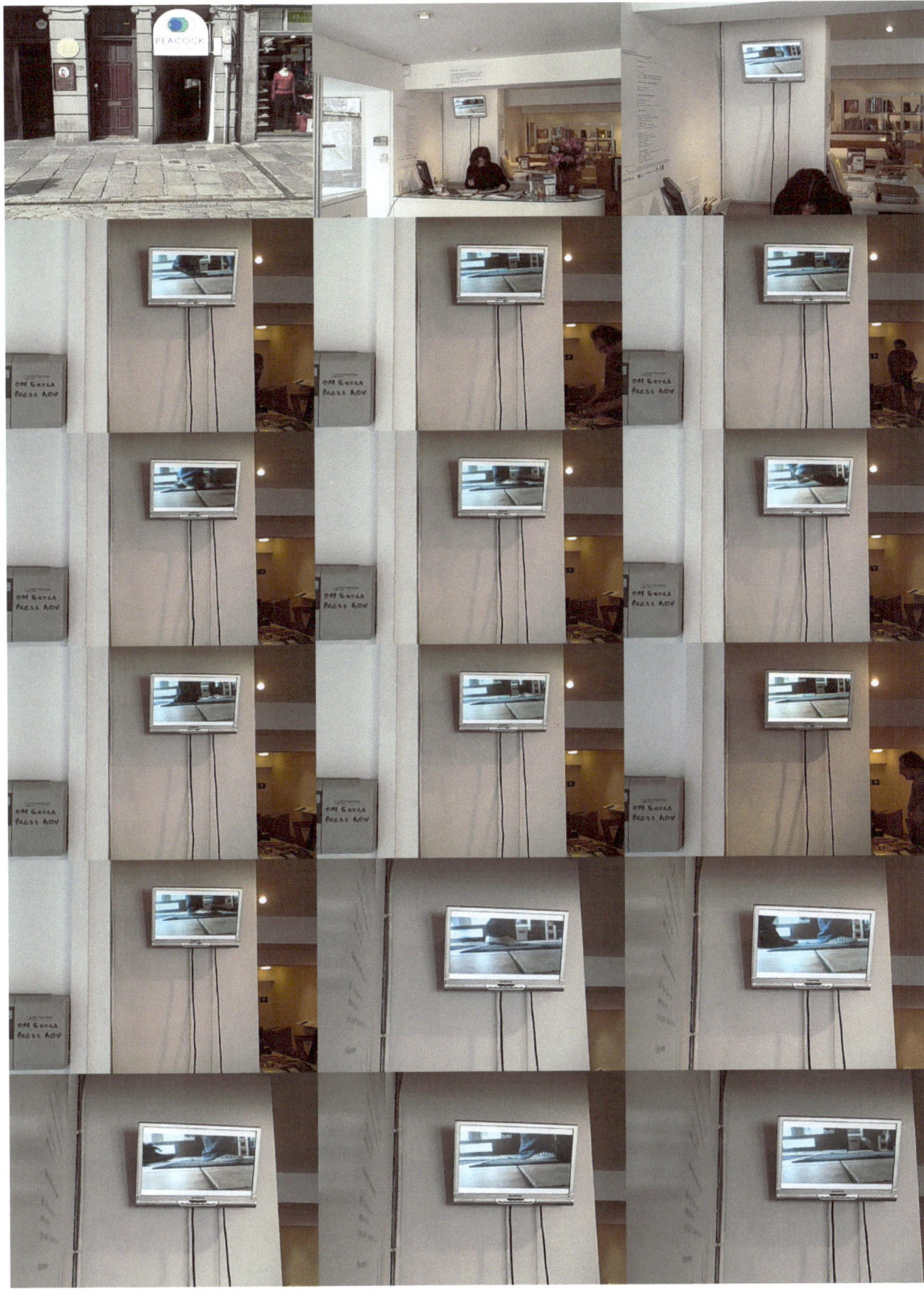

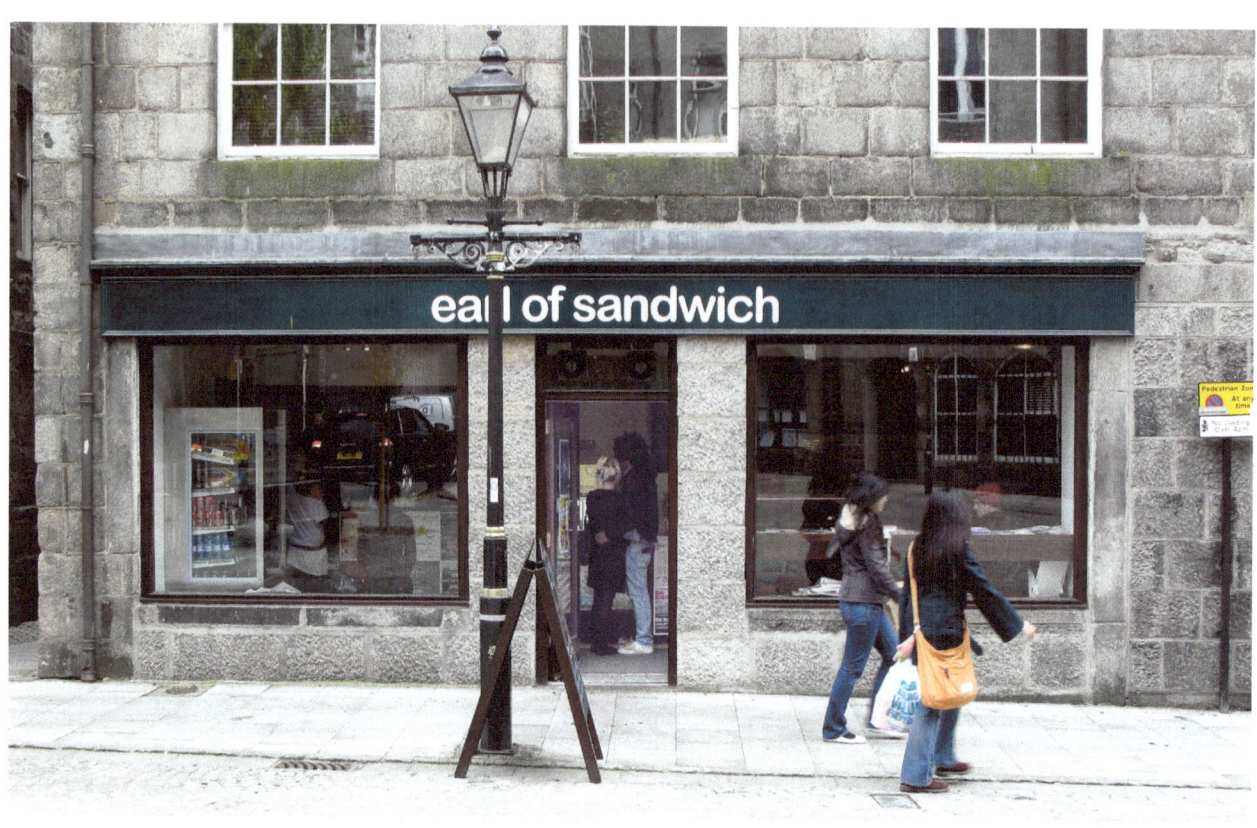

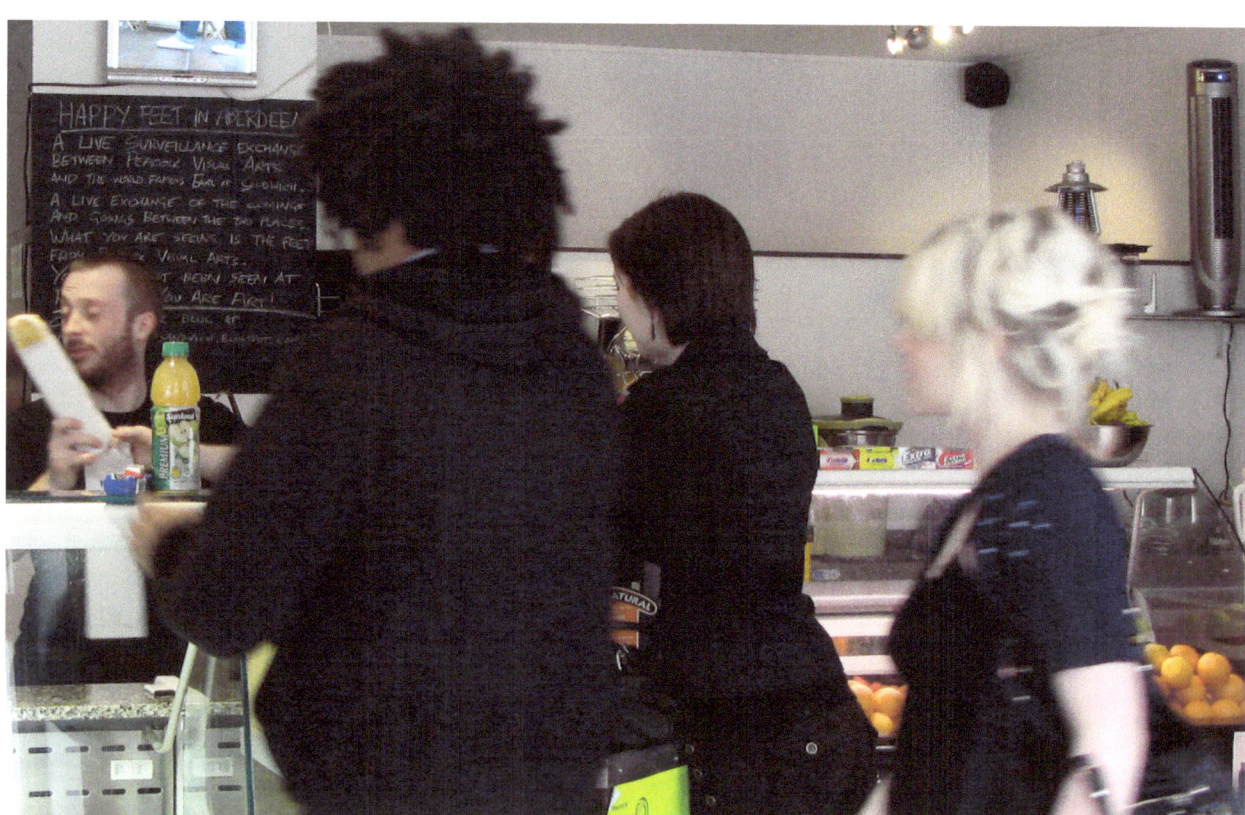

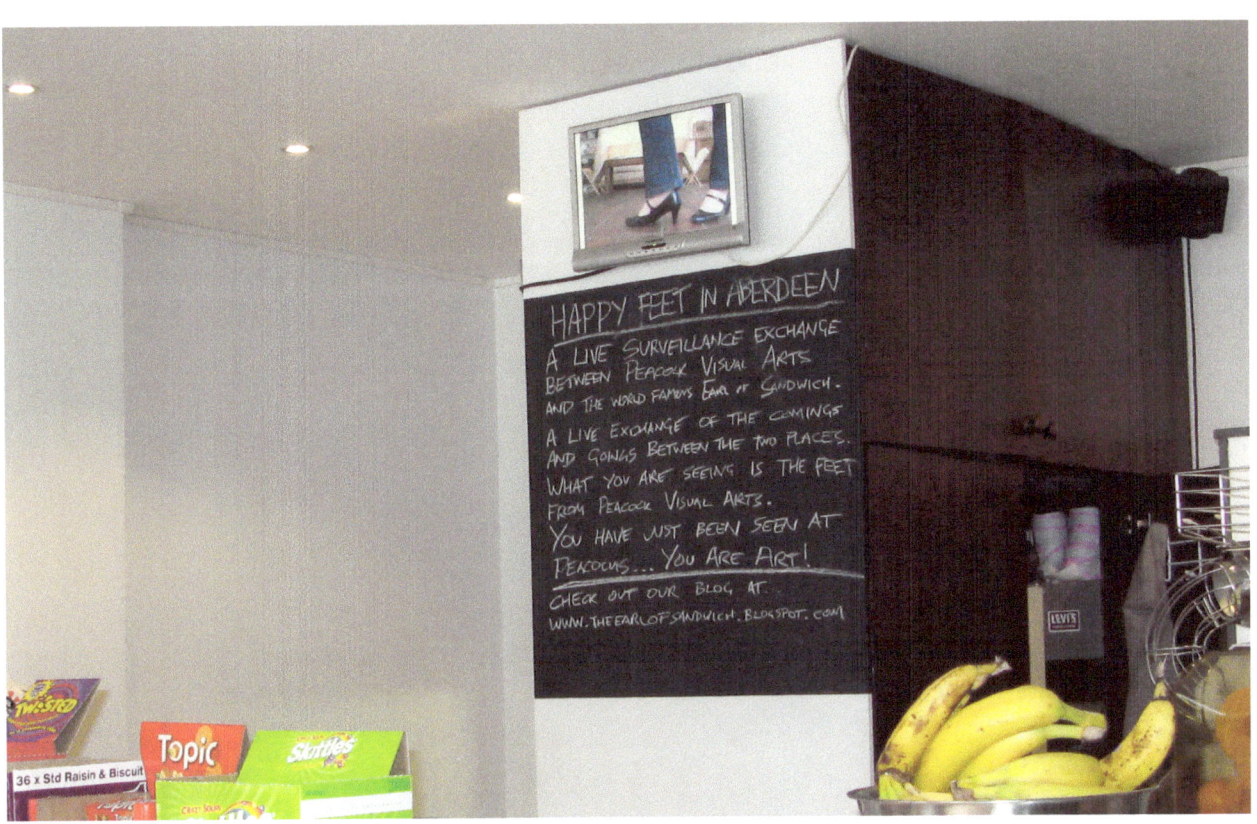

HAPPY FEET IN ABERDEEN

A LIVE SURVEILLANCE EXCHANGE
BETWEEN PEACOCK VISUAL ARTS
AND THE WORLD FAMOUS EARL of SANDWICH.
A LIVE EXCHANGE OF THE COMINGS
AND GOINGS BETWEEN THE TWO PLACES.
WHAT YOU ARE SEEING IS THE FEET
FROM PEACOCK VISUAL ARTS.
YOU HAVE JUST BEEN SEEN AT
PEACOCKS... YOU ARE ART!

CHECK OUT OUR BLOG AT.
WWW.THEEARLOFSANDWICH.BLOGSPOT.COM

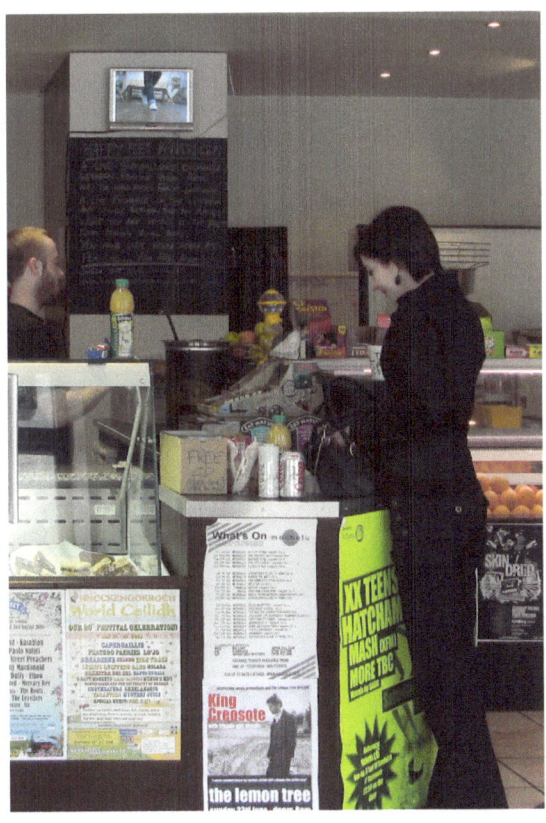

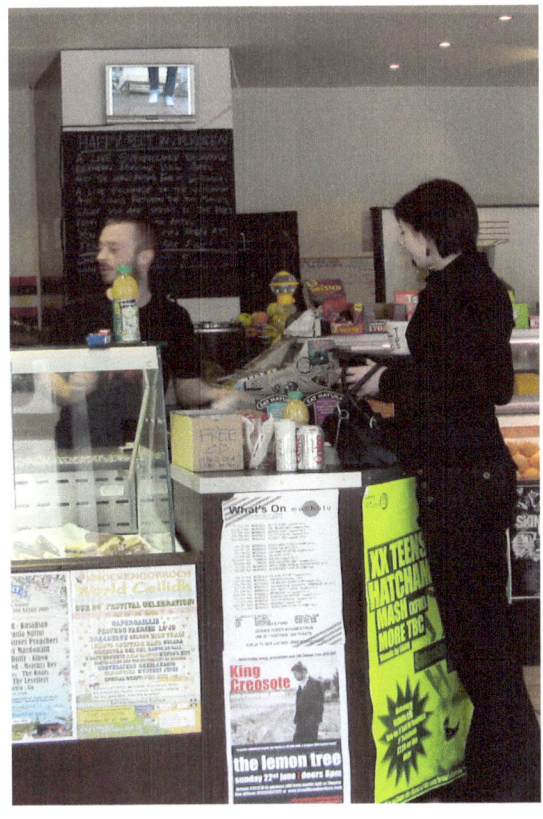

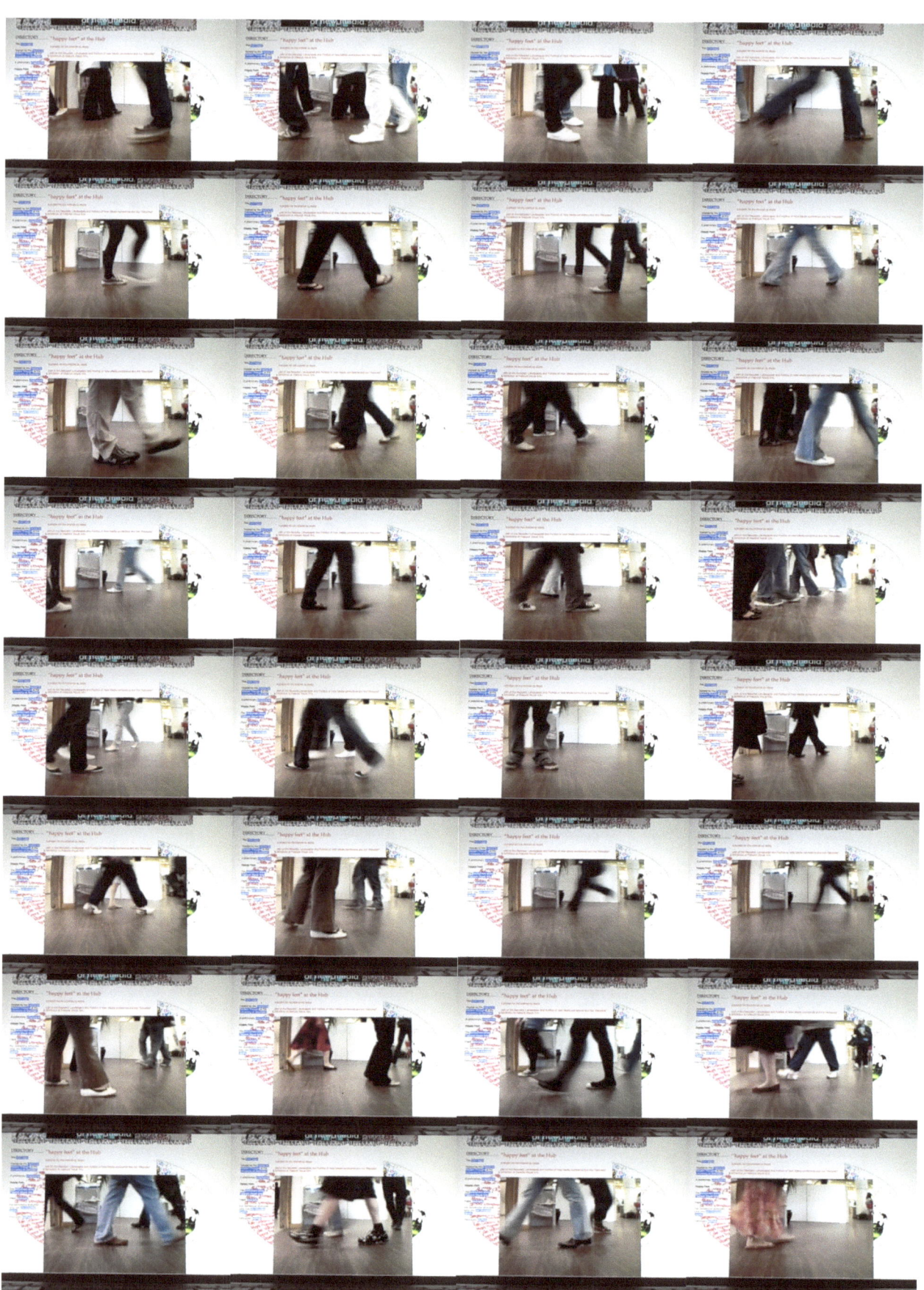

Happy Feet in Aberdeen

Part Two

University of Aberdeen cafeteria the Hub /

Recoded website and conference

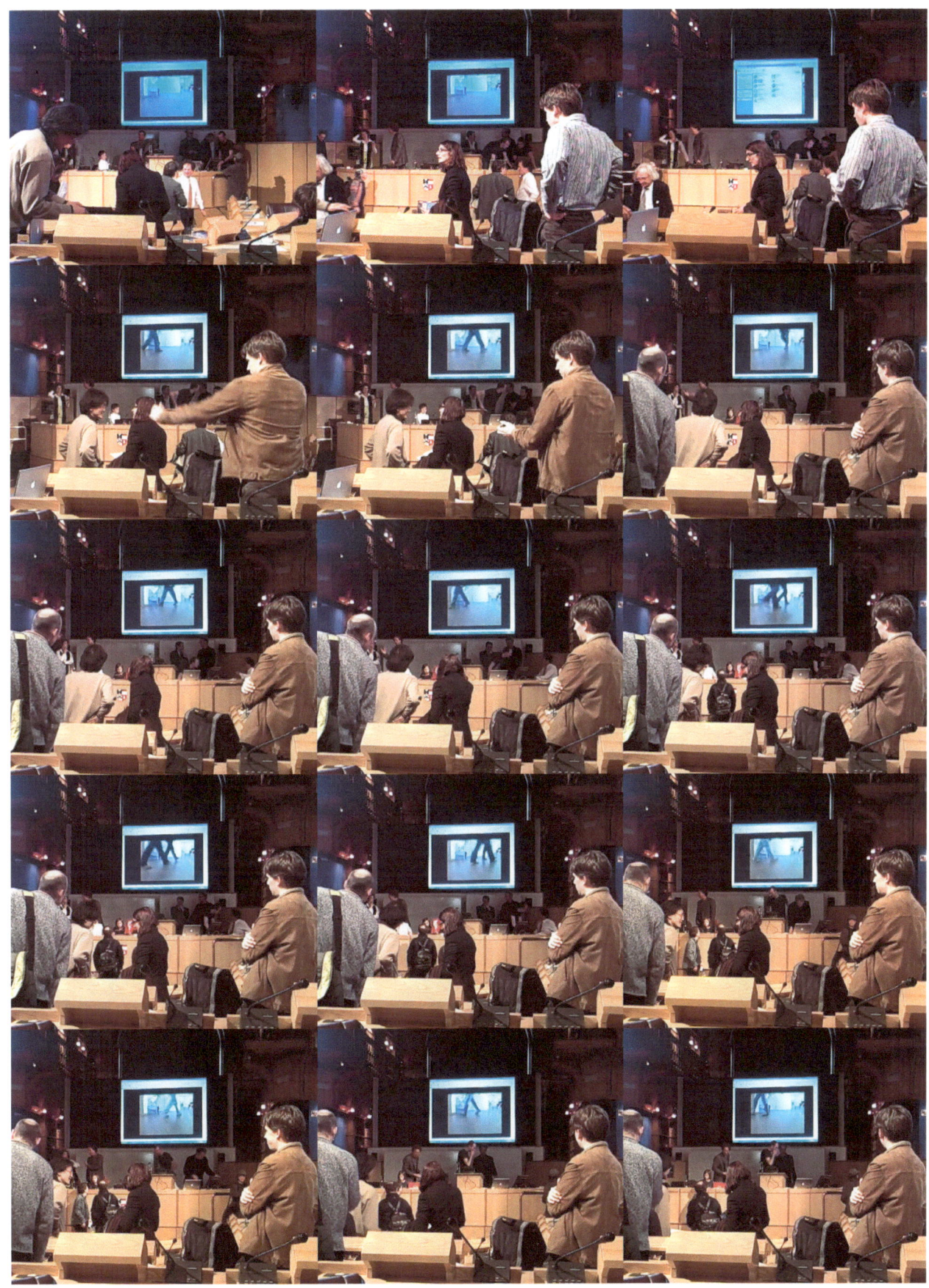

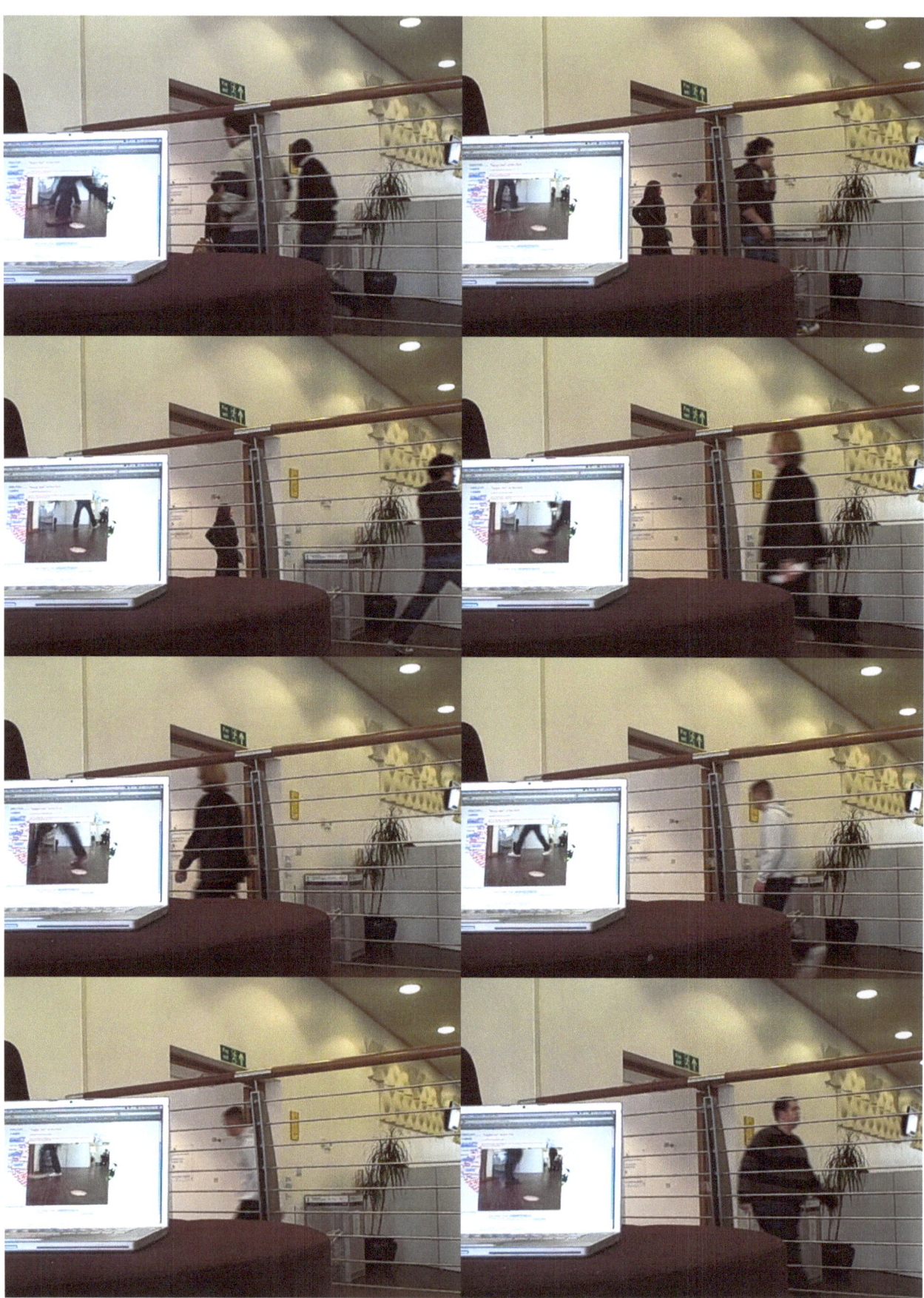

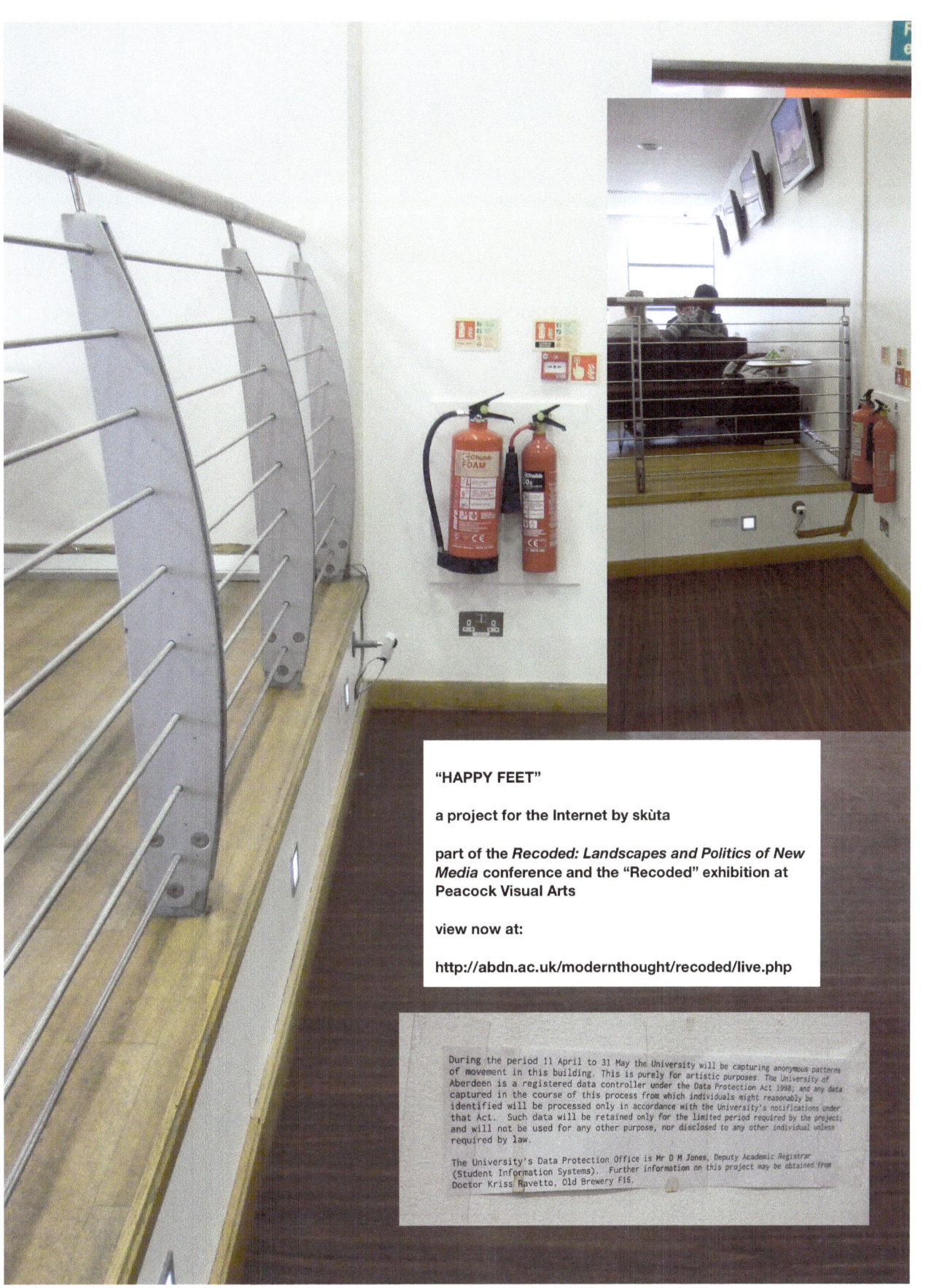

"HAPPY FEET"

a project for the Internet by skùta

part of the *Recoded: Landscapes and Politics of New Media* conference and the "Recoded" exhibition at Peacock Visual Arts

view now at:

http://abdn.ac.uk/modernthought/recoded/live.php

During the period 11 April to 31 May the University will be capturing anonymous patterns of movement in this building. This is purely for artistic purposes. The University of Aberdeen is a registered data controller under the Data Protection Act 1998; and any data captured in the course of this process from which individuals might reasonably be identified will be processed only in accordance with the University's notifications under that Act. Such data will be retained only for the limited period required by the project; and will not be used for any other purpose, nor disclosed to any other individual unless required by law.

The University's Data Protection Office is Mr D M Jones, Deputy Academic Registrar (Student Information Systems). Further information on this project may be obtained from Doctor Kriss Ravetto, Old Brewery F16.

Jens Strandberg

PowerPoint

The function of this text is to give a brief
understanding and provide documentation of my
project on PowerPoint, the work I exhibited at
Peacock Visual Arts in 2008. This short text is
written for the catalogue Peacock decided to produce
in relation to the exhibition.

My complete research on PowerPoint is difficult to
translate for this context, instead information
needs to be condensed and compromised in order to
fit the catalogue format. What is ultimately left
here is a trace of the project, functioning as a
reminder of the exhibition event in Aberdeen. The
graphical computer presentation software PowerPoint
has an ability to compress information. It enables
a speaker, with the help of a data projector, to
illustrate ideas, pinpoint information, organise
and control a digital presentation. PowerPoint is
what this work is about. It is a body of research
I carried out between 2005 and 2006 that aims to
look at the impact of the structure and language
that PowerPoint supports and how this shapes the
discourses that emerge from its use.

It draws from theoretical texts, my personal
experiences, contemporary culture and religion.
It also includes some more complex ideas relating
to knowledge production, archiving and digital
information; these subjects are so broad that each
deserve an entire project of their own in order to
fulfill a complete analysis.

Occasionally my approach can seem superficial;
this is done deliberately and can be viewed as a
ramification of the use of PowerPoint.

< Jens Strandberg >

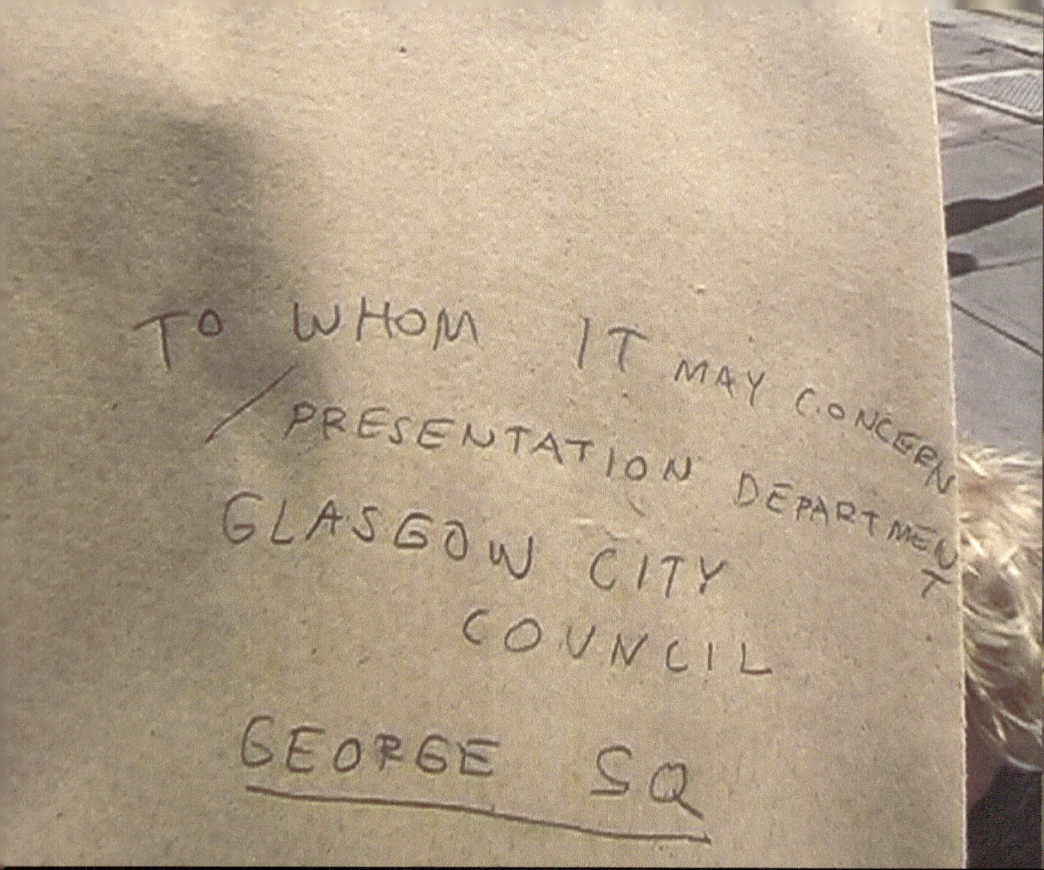

TO WHOM IT MAY CONCERN
/ PRESENTATION DEPARTMENT
GLASGOW CITY
COUNCIL

GEORGE SQ

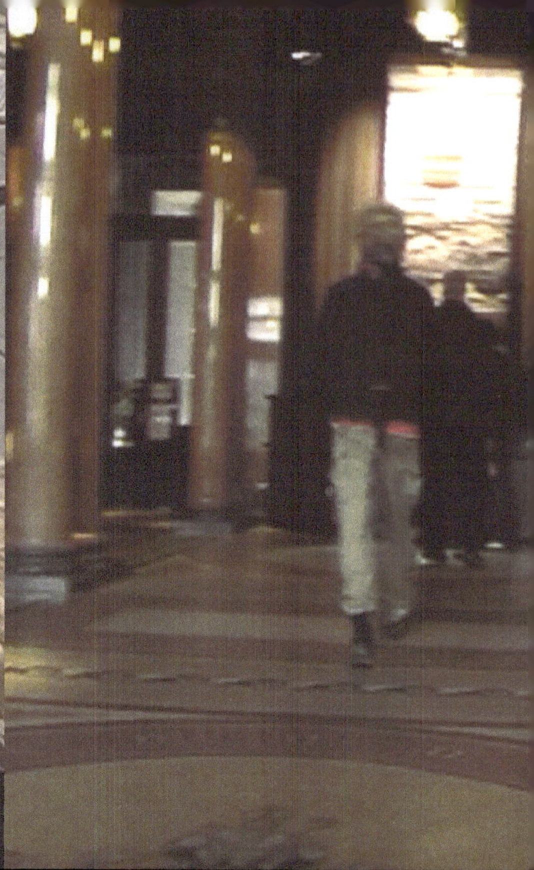

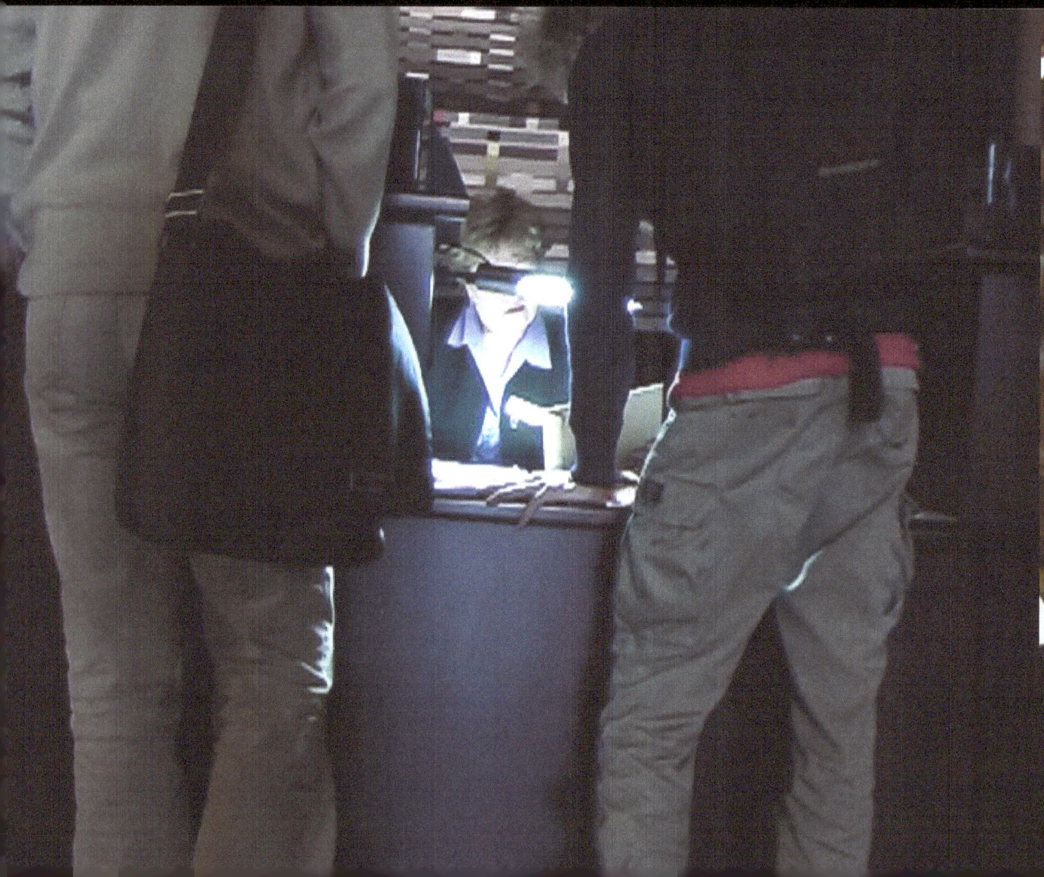

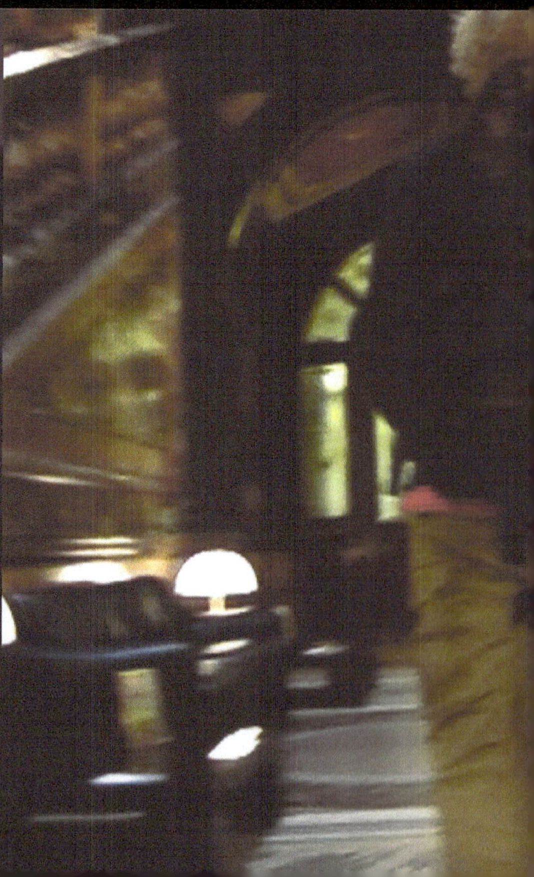

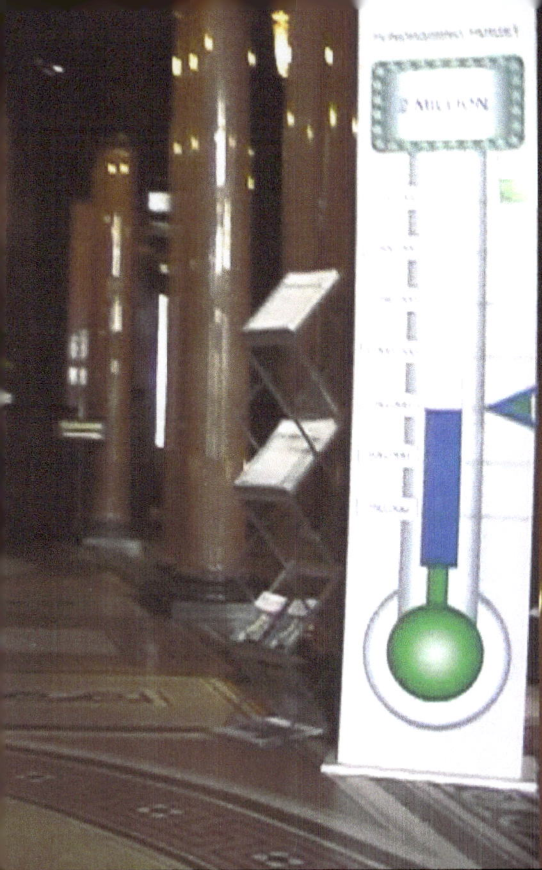
2 MILLION

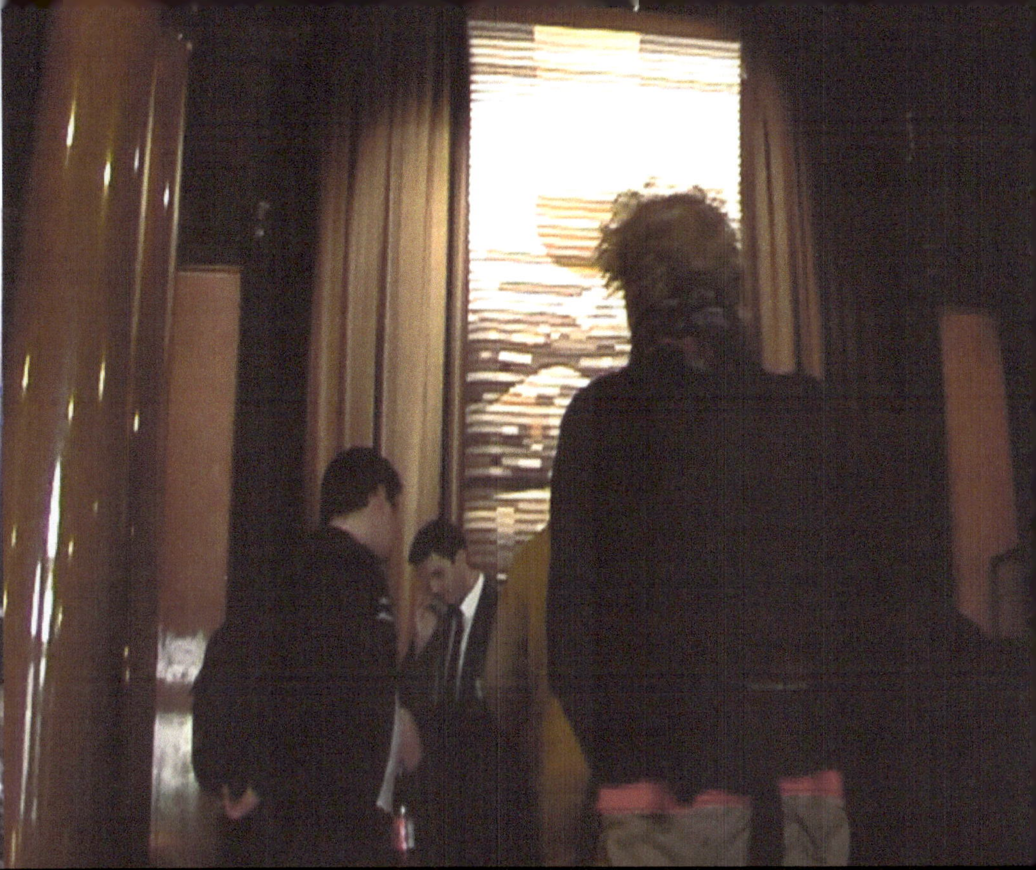

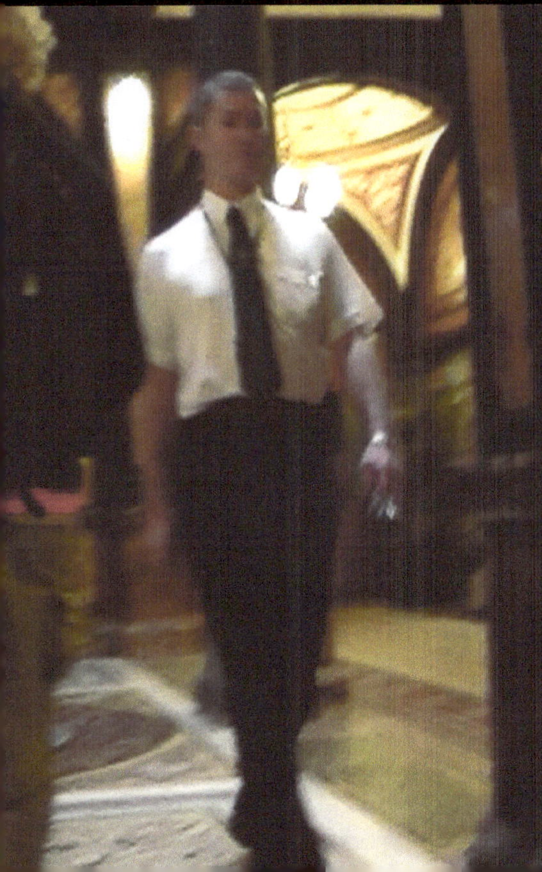

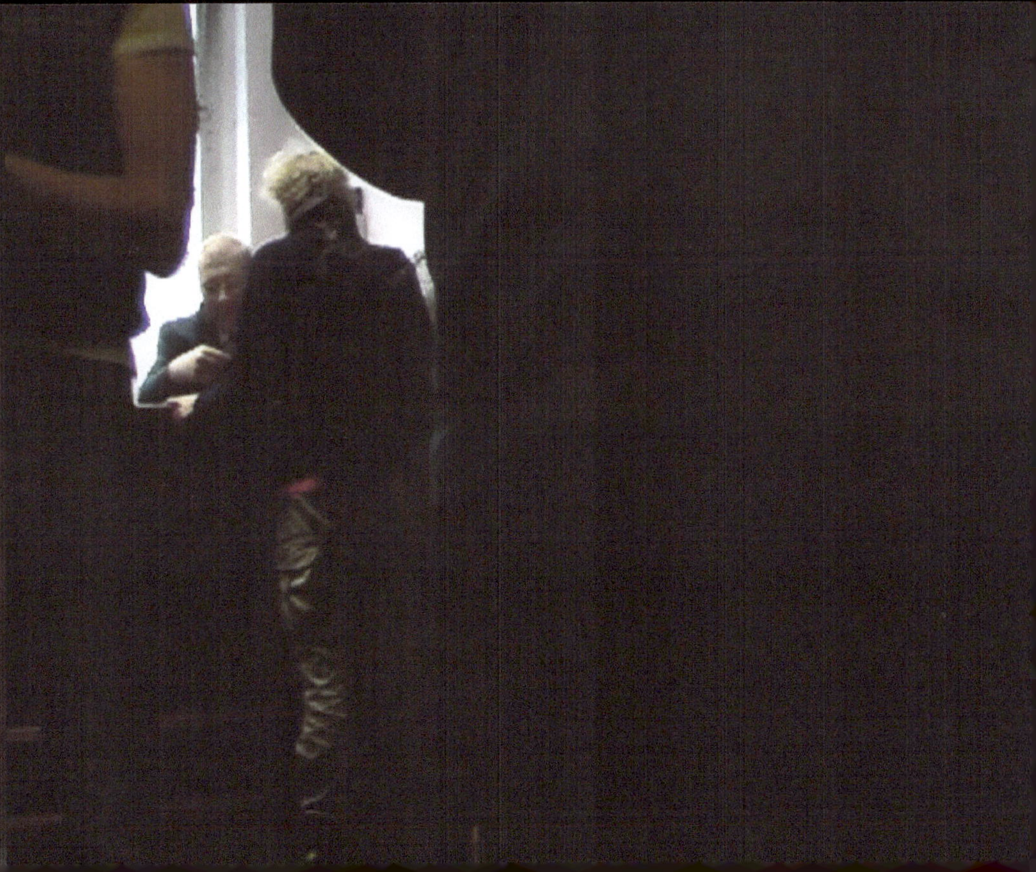

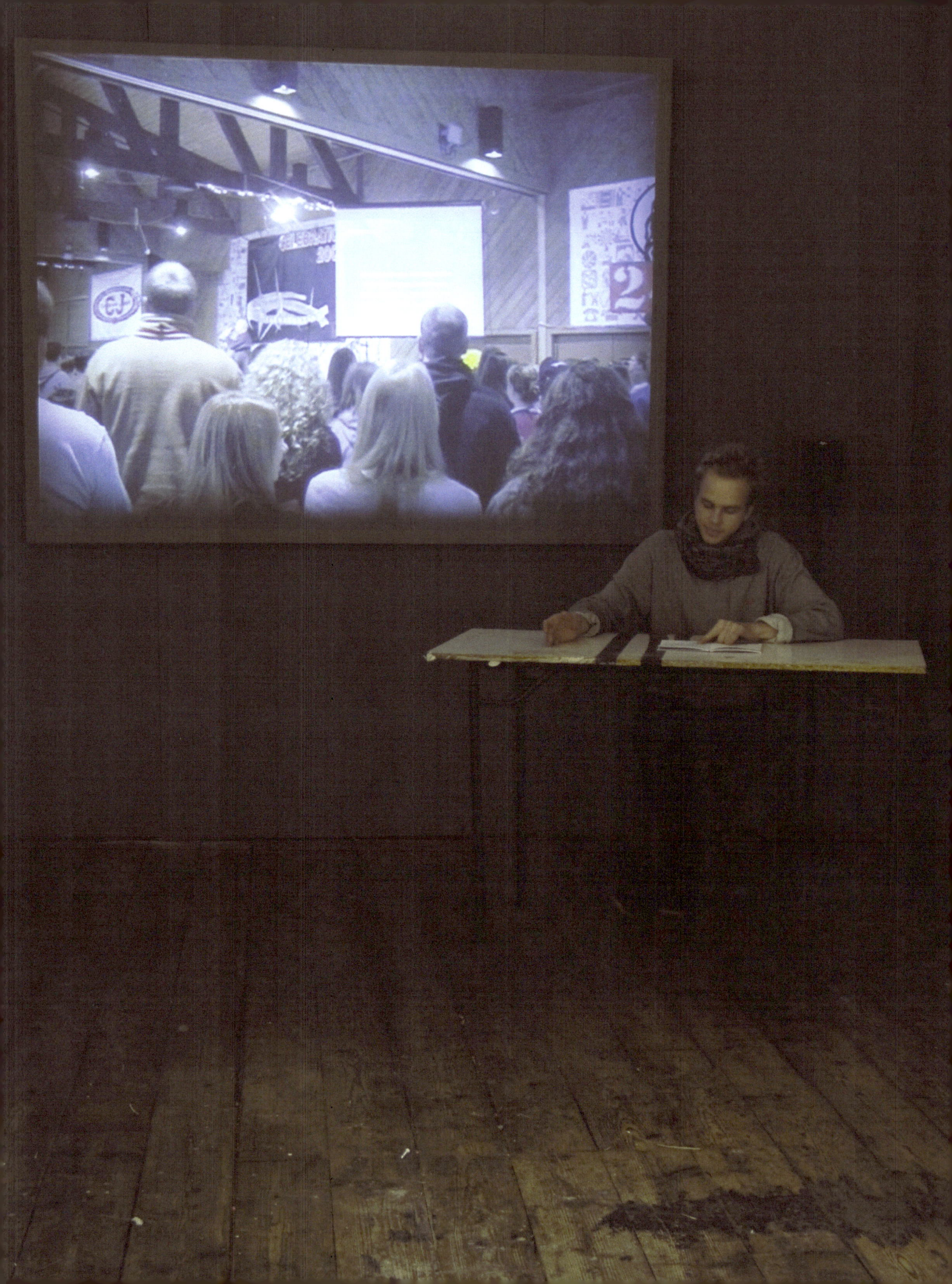

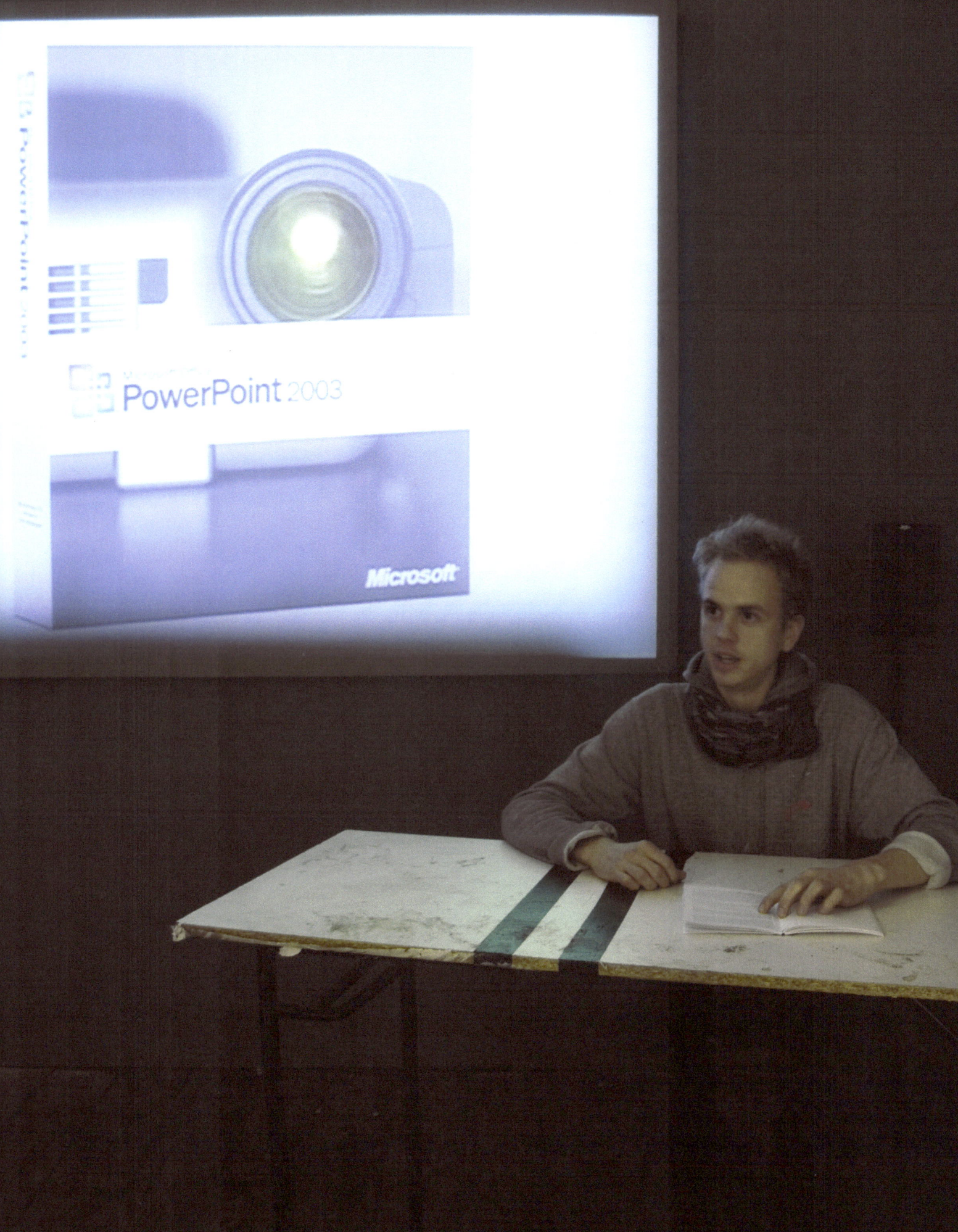

Film-screenings

FACELESS (Manu Luksch 2007)

In an eerily familiar city, a calendar reform has
dispensed with the past and the future, leaving
citizens faceless, without memory or anticipation.
Unimaginable happiness abounds – until a woman
recovers her face…
FACELESS uses recordings from the existing CCTV
networks in London, obtained under the Data
Protection Act, as "legal readymades" to construct
a strange yet plausible world. Narrated by Tilda
Swinton.

< Manu Luksch >

How Little We Know of Our Neighbours (Rebecca Baron
2005)

'How Little We Know of Our Neighbours' is an
experimental documentary about Britain's Mass
Observation Movement and its relationship to
contemporary issues regarding surveillance, public
self-disclosure, and privacy.

Images of the World and the Inscription of War
(Harun Farocki 1988)

The vanishing point of Images of The World is
the conceptual image of the 'blind spot' of the
evaluators of aerial footage of the IG Farben
industrial plant taken by the Americans in 1944.
Commentaries and notes on the photographs show that
it was only decades later that the CIA noticed
what the Allies hadn't wanted to see: that the
Auschwitz concentration camp is depicted next to the
industrial bombing target. (At one point during this
later investigation, the image of an experimental
wave pool - already visible at the beginning of
the film - flashes across the screen, recognizably
referring to the biding of the gaze: for one's gaze
and thoughts are not free when machines, in league
with science and the military, dictate what is to be
investigated. Farocki thereby puts his finger on the
essence of media violence, a "terrorist aesthetic"
(Paul Virilio) of optic stimulation, which today
appears on control panels as well as on television,
with its admitted goal of making the observer into
either an accomplice or a potential victim, as in
times of war.

< Christa Blümlinger >

Secrecy (Peter Galison and Robb Moss 2007)

In a single recent year the U.S. classified about five
times the number of pages added to the Library of
Congress. We live in a world where the production
of secret knowledge dwarfs the production of open
knowledge By focusing on classified secrets, the
government's ability to put information out of sight
if it would harm national security, Secrecy explores
the tensions between the safety of the nation, and
its ability to function as a democracy.

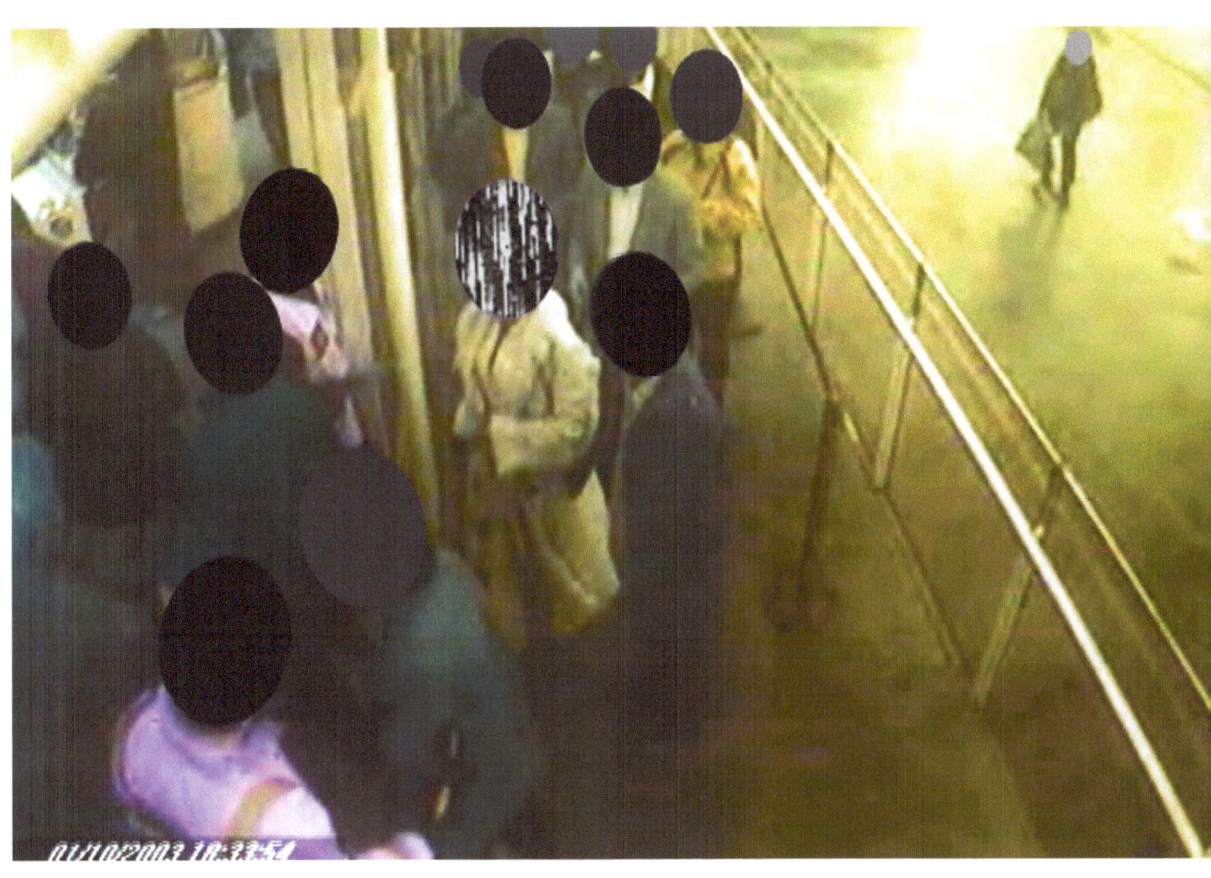

Manu Luksch. Search She
Still from FACELESS
Courtesy AMOUR FOU & Ambient Information Systems

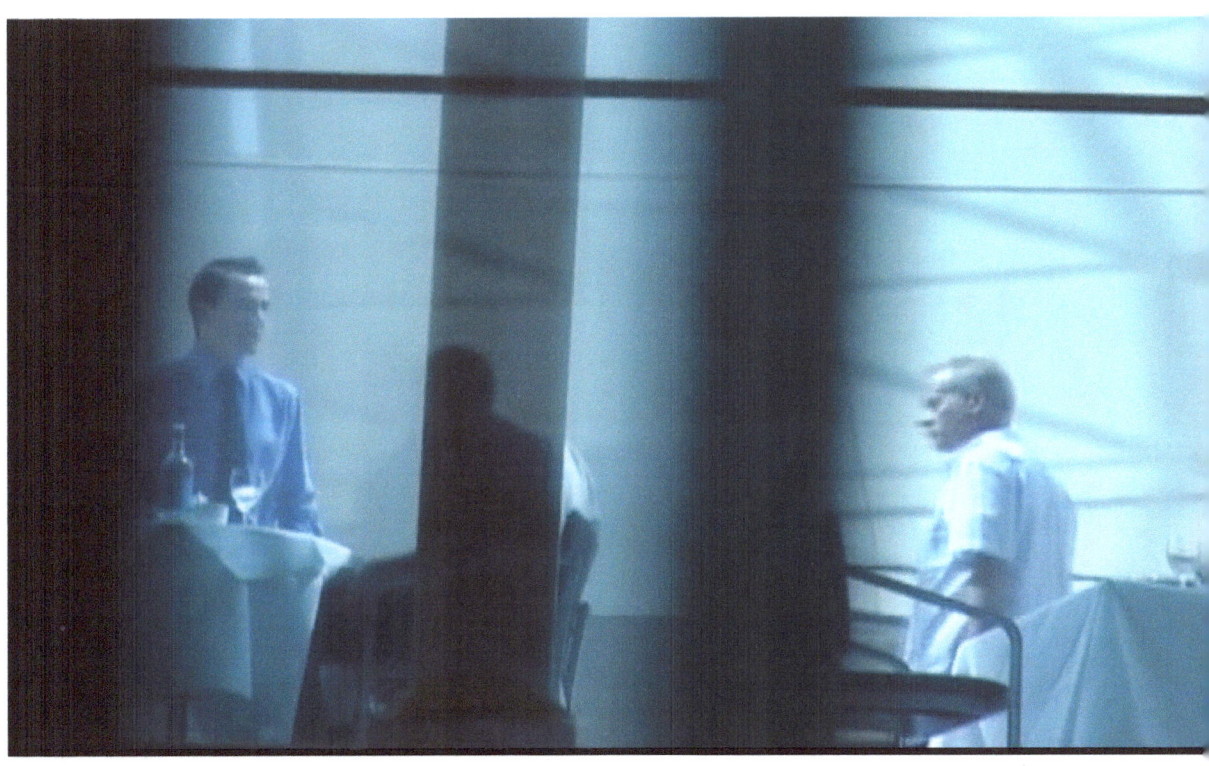

Still from How Little We Know of Our Neighbours
Courtesy Video Data Bank, Chicago

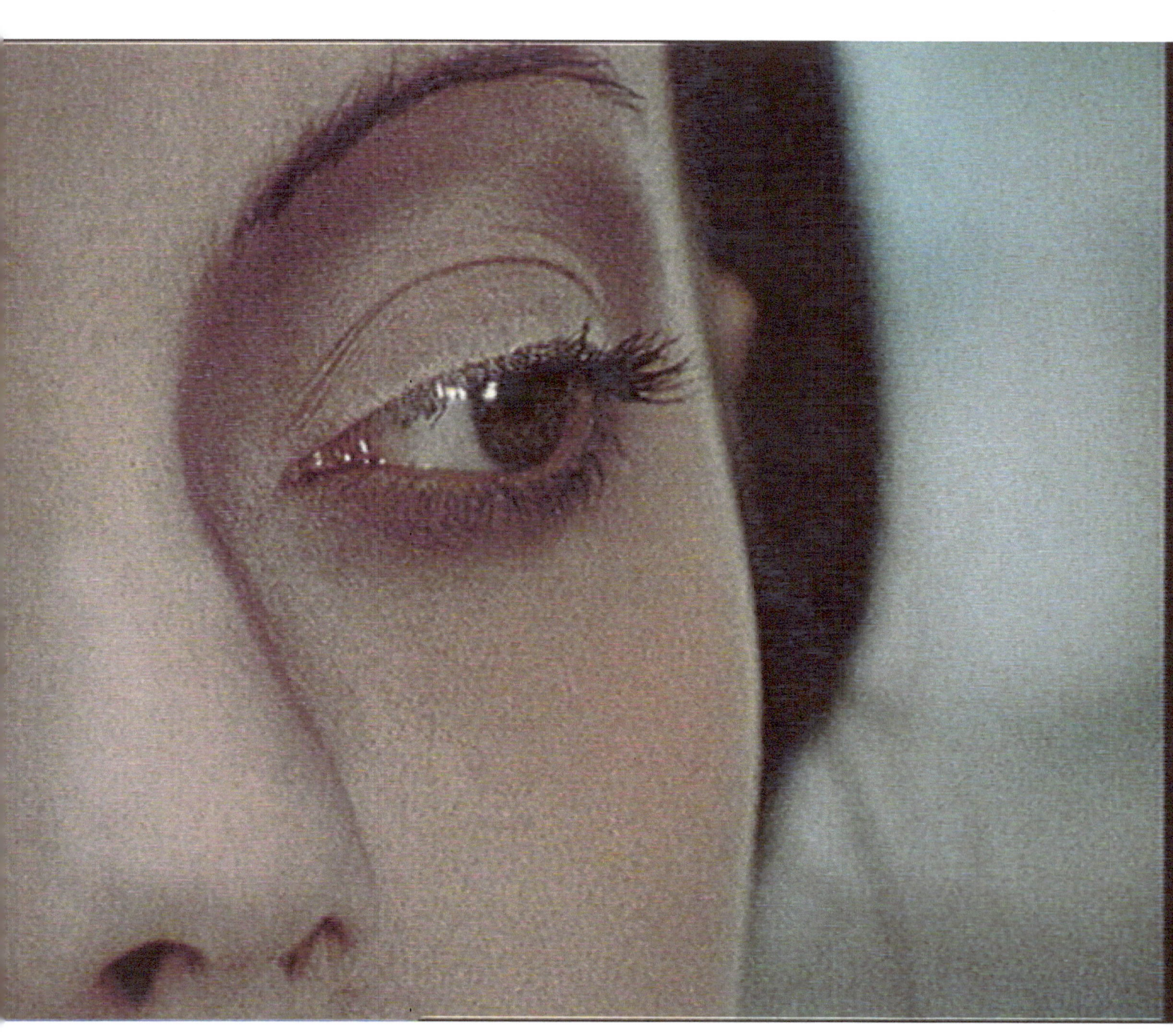

Still from Images of the World and the Inscription of War.
Courtesy Harun Farocki Filmproduktion

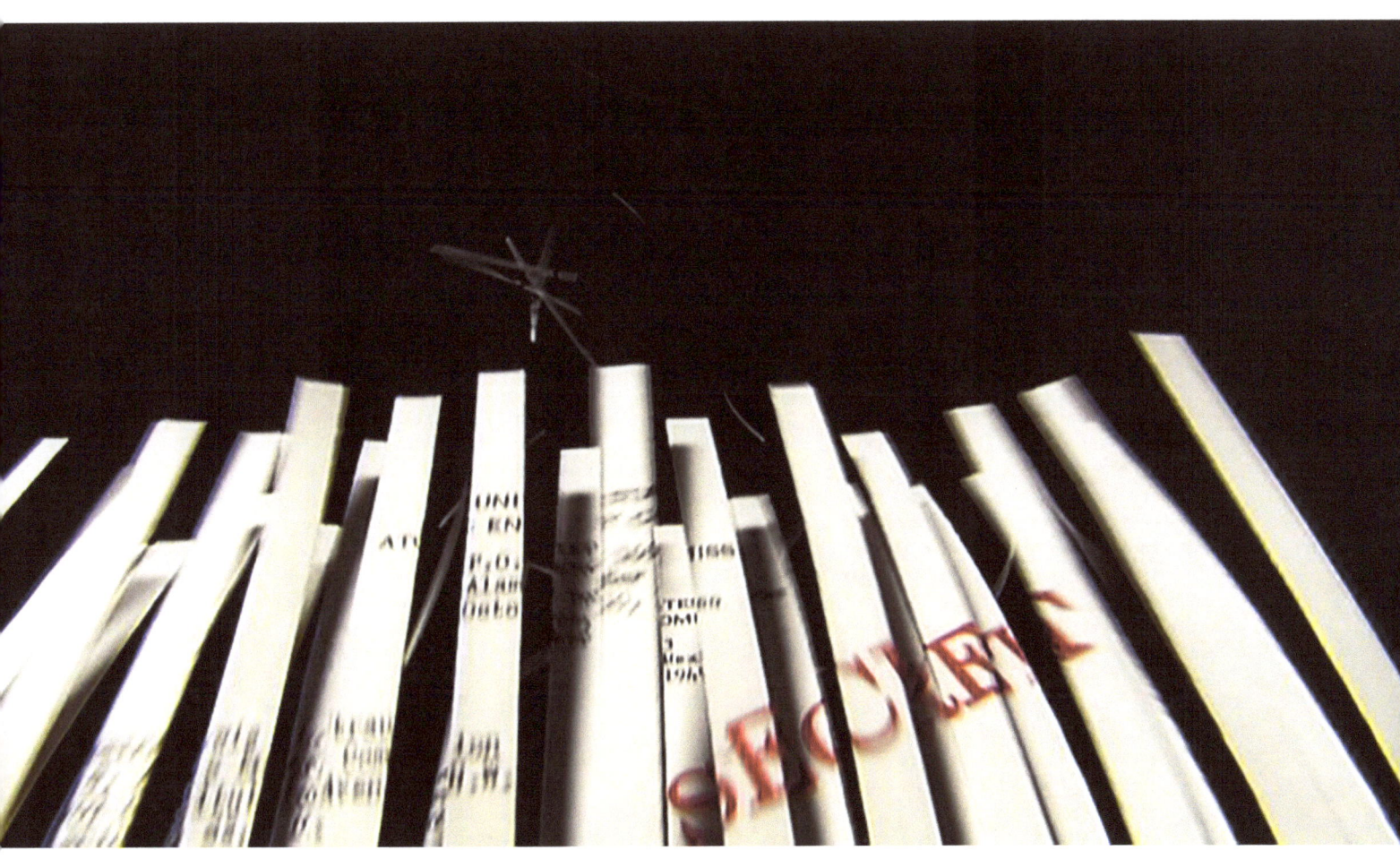

Still from Secrecy
Courtesy Secrecy Film Project

Contributors

Jay Murphy is a writer living in Aberdeen, Scotland and sometimes New York. He has contributed to *Parkett, Contemporary, Metropolis, Art in America, Afterimage, Frieze,* and many other journals. His screenplay Vesco was a finalist for the Sundance Screenwriting Labs, and his collaborative Internet projects have been shown in the Sundance Online Film Festival. He is currently organizing gallery exhibitions in New York and Edinburgh and completing a doctoral dissertation at the Centre for Modern Thought/University of Aberdeen.

Alexander Egger is an Italian graphic designer, illustrator, concept developer, artist, writer and musician, currently living and working in Vienna and sometimes elsewhere. Can't drive even though he has got a driving license. Doesn't like vegetables. Is dreaming frequently of plane crashes lately. Has plenty of useless knowledge about a lot of things nobody is interested in. Likes people sometimes. Loves the phase between sleep and alertness when thoughts and images come to one's mind from nowhere in a half aware accidental order compounding to strange combinations. Reads mostly 4-5 books at the same time and in a fast rotation. Had his work exposed in every continent in the last year except Antarctica. A monograph of his work with the title: Satellites Mistaken for Stars will be available at Gingko Press soon.

Anna Jermolaewa, born in St. Petersburg, Russia in 1970, has been living in Vienna, Austria, since 1989. In 1998 she graduated in History of Art from the University of Vienna, in 2002 in Painting & Graphic Art / New Media from the Academy of Fine Arts in Vienna . Since 2005 she is Professor for Media Arts, State School of Design / ZKM Karlsruhe, Germany. In her video works, photography and paintings, Anna Jermolaewa concentrates on the analysis of manipulation and power structures in current society and its efffects on individuals. Ass Peeping also exists as a limited edtion artist's book: onestar press, Paris 2003.

Caleb Larsen is from Michigan, USA, and is currently studying for an MFA in Digital + Media at the Rhode Island School of Design. He has a Bachelor of Fine Arts in Painting from Western Michigan University. He has exhibited in New York, Los Angeles, San Francisco, Detroit, Canada, Greece and Romania. He attended the Yale Norfolk Summer School of Art, the School of Visual Art Artist Residency, and most recently the I-Park Artist Residency in Connecticut. His work is concerned with using logic-based systems to create and explore intersections of digital and physical culture using Language and Mapping as methods of inspection.

Manu Luksch, founder of the London-based arts production company ambientTV.NET, studied Fine Arts in Vienna and Thailand, before joining the the Media Lab Munich as Artistic Director (1995-97). AmbientTV.NET conceives and produces interdisciplinary and collaborative projects, ranging in form from installation through documentary, dance, and gastronomy, to sound and video composition and live manipulation; techniques and effects of live data broadcasting and transmission provide theme, medium, and performative space for many of the works. Projects are shown at venues and festivals internationally, such as in "Connecting Worlds" (NTT ICC, Tokyo 2006), "Custom Living" (BK Gallery, Sydney 2006), "Satellite of Love" (Witte de With, Rotterdam 2006), Ars Electronica (Linz 2005, 2007), to name the most recent.

David Valentine experiments with modern technologies to find new ways of applying them to the content and meaning of film. He has produced nationally distributed and award winning short films and regularly writes for international independent film magazine Showreel. MediaShed is the first 'free-media' space to open in the East of England. It's a place for doing art, making things or just saying what you want for little or no financial cost by using the public domain, free software, recycled equipment and enthusiasm.

Trevor Paglen is an artist, writer, and experimental geographer working out of the Department of Geography at the University of California, Berkeley. His work involves deliberately blurring the lines between social science, contemporary art, and a host of even more obscure disciplines in order to construct unfamiliar, yet meticulously researched ways to interpret the world around us. His most recent projects involve close examinations of state secrecy, the California prison system, and the CIA's practice of "extraordinary rendition." Paglen holds a BA from UC Berkeley, an MFA from the School of the Art Institute of Chicago, and is currently completing a PhD in the Department of Geography at the University of California at Berkeley.

plan b are the artists Sophia New and Daniel Belasco Rogers. They perform together under the name plan b and collaborate on each other's solo works ever since receiving Artsadmin Artists' Bursaries in 2001. plan b make sited works and location-specific performances. They make durational works which explore the dynamics of conversation, singing, confessing and cycling. Alongside their performances they have made locative media pieces, audio guides, installations, web streams, workshops, videos and

radio pieces. Daniel Belasco Rogers and Sophia New
live and work in Berlin and London.

RYbN are a multi-field artistic collective based
in Paris and Barcelona. They specialise in the
realisation of installations, performances and
interfaces by referring to the codified systems of
artistic representation – painting, architecture,
counter-cultures – as well as to human and physical
phenomena – geopolitics, socio-economy, sensory
perception, cognitive systems. The axis of their
research is the construction of a 'semantics of
convergence' through the coupling, the diversion
and the perversion of writing and formalization
tools connected to technologies of communication,
information and the sensory – webs, data flows,
smell, surveillance, audiovisual, interaction, real
time.

skúta artist at large lives and works in New York.
Originally from Iceland, he studied time-based media
with a specialization in photography and artists
books at Visual Studies Workshop in Rochester.
Since the 1980s he has participated in numerous
solo and group exhibitions internationally, as well
as producing artist books. skúta's work forms an
on-going exploration of different modes and truth-
values of diaristic documentation in any media.

Jens Strandberg, born 1980 in Örnsköldsvik/Sweden,
lives and works in Glasgow. He began his work on
Poweropoint as part of his degree in Sculpture/
Environmental Art at Glasgow School of Art,
graduating in 2007. Previously he also studied
at the Academy of Fine Arts, Vienna, Austria. He
is also involved in Draw or Die, a group which
organises drawing events, and in the music promoter
collective Nuts and Seeds. In his research Jens
Strandberg focuses on how dreams and fantasies are
formed in society and how they form associations to
power structures. He deals with this by connecting
and disconnecting materials, which may appear
disjointed. Jens also addresses the condition of a
creative process and is thus not afraid of letting
go of the original idea. The work is often time/
space specific and set up as dryly and as simple as
possible, with just the necessary devises, often
with the intention to involve the viewer in the
work.

Recoded
Landscapes and Politics of New Media.

Peacock Visual Arts in collaboration with the Centre
for Modern Thought at the University of Aberdeen.
24 April - 31 May 2008

Curated by Jack Keenan and Monika Vykoukal

Conference : Recoded. Landscapes and Politics of New
Media. 25-26 April 2008, The Centre for Modern Thought,
University of Aberdeen [Kriss Ravetto-Biagioli, Mario
Biagioli, Chris Fynsk]

Peacock Visual Arts
21 Castle Street
Aberdeen AB11 5BQ
peacockvisualarts.com
Charity SC 56235

Published by Peacock Visual Arts, Aberdeen, Scotland
Editor | Monika Vykoukal
Essay | Jay Murphy
Photographs | The Artists, Peacock Visual Arts,
David Valentine / MediaShed : Jan Dixon &
Emily Dixon < www.andthewardrobe.co.uk >,
Trevor Paglen : Bellwether Gallery, New York
Design | Scott Masser

ISBN 978 0 9555524 4 1

Peacock Visual Arts Team
Director | Lindsay Gordon
Curator | Monika Vykoukal
Assistant Curator | Angela Lennon
Press and Marketing | Nina Eggens
Printmaking | Michael Waight, Linsay Croall
Digital | Adam Proctor
Digital Assistant | Sean Fraser
3sixty-tv | Jack Keenan
Darkroom Technician | Nicole Plumb
Framing | David McCracken, Mark McCracken
Gallery Assistant | Dana Swanson
Accounts | Alison Kennedy
Factota | Sandy Simpson, Douglas Colvin

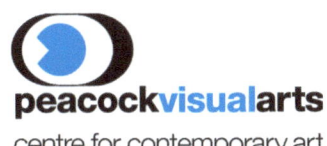
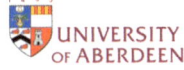
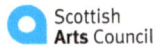
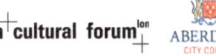

www.ingramcontent.com/pod-product-compliance
Lightning Source LLC
Chambersburg PA
CBHW050732180526
45159CB00003B/1202